MW00779376

Basket Case: An argument for crazy.

First Edition published August 22nd, 2024

ISBN 979-8-9909838-0-9 (paperback)

IBSN 979-8-9909838-8-5 (hardback)

Bunni Ambrosia

www.shiftwithbunni.com

Printed in the USA

CONTENTS

For L., P., and C.

– MY FAVORITE EGGS.

INTRODUCTION

Hi. I'm the problem. It's me, Bunni.

My life is a tapestry of contradictions. From a 17-year-old dropout, widowed mother, and recovering addict, I've evolved into a neurodivergent adult. This book is not just about my journey but also about the strategies I've mastered to achieve my goals. I've worn many hats, and I thrive on learning new skills. I aspire to be a master of all trades, and I'm well on my way.

I have endeavored to find a way to make my life work in many, many.... many ways. I rarely feel like I know what I'm doing, but I try to do the best that I can with what I have at the time. And at times, that wasn't much. There were a few years that I was raising a child on roughly $12000 a year. Though my efforts may be considered "unconventional", I am proud of all the roads I have traveled to find this formula to success that has become the Basket Case method with which I teach my coaching clientele. And yet, I am even more grateful to be able to share this "elusive secret" with you. (Spoiler alert... it's no secret.) My sincerest hope is that you, too, may find a path to your own personal victories using these skills and techniques.

Let me share some of my experiences, past and present, with you. There are so many sides to me. I am a Mama and a father. A daughter. Sister. Widow and wife. A woman. Man enough. A friend of Dorothy. An unwilling only child. A foster child. A ward of the state. A dropout. A graduate. A birthmother. A drug addict. An urban farmer. An unschooler. A server. Housekeeper. A roofer. Teller. A steak dinner delivery driver. A health insurance agent licensed in all 50 states. A barista. A stay-at-home parent. An Activist. An artist. A questioner. An abolitionist. Writer. Advocate. Sexual being. I am a chronic illness patient and a caregiver. I am a trucker and a vegan. A reverend and an atheist. An athlete. A hugger. An end-of-life doula. A dog lover. An auDHDer. A student. A bookworm. I am, as of 2020, an entrepreneur and now an author. Plainly, I want to do "all the things". If you are reading this book, chances are you also want to experience all that life has to offer, too, or you're my editor. In the case of the latter, I do apologize for my dyslexic self. *Insert shrug here*

A lot has happened since I finished this book the first time. I got divorced, discovered that I have ADHD and autism, and my beloved Daddio left this world. These events have each given me new perspectives on various areas of my life. Because of this fresh insight, I have gone back, updated a few thoughts in this book, and added a story or two that is relatable. I appreciate you joining me on this journey of growth and continuation of seeing the possibilities around us. I'm literally sitting in my camp chair in the Colorado River near Blythe, CA, as I write this intro. Thank goodness for "water-resistant" devices. I am eternally grateful for the privileges I've been granted in this life. As a trucker, I'm paid to travel to beautiful places and forced to take time for myself. Today that means spending my free time as submerged as possible because it's 121°F. The mile walk from the truck stop to the river felt akin to a stroll through a crematorium. The wind-sun combo is like walking face-first into a giant blow dryer. The 86°F water and shade beneath the i10 bridge is the perfect respite on this lazy Sunday. Today I am rejoicing in my blessings and remembering the rough roads that lead to this happiness. It hasn't always been this easy to be grateful. My father gifted me with many things, not the least of which is the courage to step forward daily.

I love trying new things and taking big risks, and I am afraid of the "next step". As Georgia O'Keeffe said, "I've been absolutely terrified every moment of my life – and I've never let it keep me from doing a single thing I wanted to do.". I simply refuse to allow fear to stop me from taking any of the steps along my path. My sweet daughter has heard me say, "It's okay to be afraid. It's not okay to let that stop you." There have been too many times for me to be allowed to indulge my fears. In this book, I intend to show you why you, too, should run face-first into your fears as if your life depended on it. Run as hard as you can toward your dreams. I promise you will reach them if you follow the steps listed throughout this book. You will learn how to calibrate your internal compass and specifically define your next steps. Contrary to popular belief, you will see why it is imperative to put all your eggs in one basket at a time. Yes. All of them. Reaching your goals is an "all or nothing" sport. You must go all in for YOURSELF. Believe first. The rest will line up.

The title of this book is Basket Case. This implies a bit of insanity is necessary, and it's true. Sort of. I am a total basket case and I hope you'll join me as such. Many of those around you will be all too happy to tell you that you are crazy. You'll never reach *that* goal. And definitely do not put your all into one thing. You need a backup plan. What if you fail? Some may even literally say, "Don't put all of your eggs in one basket." They will often be offering what they think is helpful, sound advice. Politely, tell them to bug off. Seriously though, consider the ideas in this book before making the same "safe bet" with mediocrity they have made. No shade to them, but you want more out of life than ordinary, right? Remember taking no risks is the biggest risk of all.

This book will show you how doing quite the opposite is the recipe for success. I would like to postulate that you should put every single egg in your basket. Once you have filled your basket, or accomplished your goal, start a new basket. Throughout this book, we will examine the Who, the Why, the What, and the How of your goals. We'll take a look at the self behind your masks, what makes you move, the tools required to achieve success as you've only dreamed thus far, and cartograph out the map to get you across the finish lines of your life. You will learn how to reach any goal you set your mind to while honoring your authentic self.

I am taking my own advice right now. I have written and rewritten every page in this book. My perfectionism has gotten the better of me numerous times since I began this journey. There is a voice in my head telling me to push back the publish date. To keep working on it and lying to me. The voice is telling me that I am not enough and that this book isn't enough either. Well, you little goblin in my head. It's got to be good enough for now, and that is all that matters. I can write a Basket Case 2.0 later if I feel the need.

Thank you for reading and supporting me throughout this entire process. And most importantly, thank you for allowing me to be human too. I hope you enjoy my stories and are able to take away something that moves you a step closer to the person you want to be. Skoden!

"Don't put all your eggs in one basket." –

A well-meaning but misinformed old man.

Probably.

Personal Mission Statement

It is my mission to live gently by seeking the positive in all things, to facilitate growth; to hold space for and honor the value of all others; to give to my communities in time and treasure; and to use my knowledge and dedication to excellence to lift others into their own light.

BASKET CASE

CHAPTER 1- BEGINNINGS

Alright, here we go. As Mark Twain said, "The secret of getting ahead is getting started.". It certainly has been the most difficult part of writing this book. So far, anyway. (Thankfully, that bit only took about 3 years. Here's to hoping the rest goes somewhat faster.) Starting out always seems to be the hardest part of anything meaningful in life, doesn't it? Writing this book certainly has seemed that way to me and I sincerely hope that you can also take something meaningful from within these pages.

This work intends to assist you in conquering your goals consistently. This is not the "you just need to be more passionate to succeed" book. We both already know you are plenty passionate. You would not have reached for this book if that were not the case. Let me first say yakoke ("thank you") for bringing your fire to this space. I am beyond excited to see all that you bring to this world by becoming a basket case, too. Within these pages, I will show you how to define your own path and utilize the skills you already possess to make real and lasting progress in your life.

 Over the years and through the many struggles of my life, imagining my dreams and successes has never been the problem. I could daydream for hours. Have you ever struggled to dream about what you will do when you "make it"? I didn't think so. The trouble has always been in finding the path between having the dream and bringing it to fruition. In the past, I would often become overwhelmed by the distance between where I was and where I wanted to be, so I couldn't even imagine the steps to get there. It was as if my dreams were on top of a sheer cliff. It took longer than I'd like to admit to find the staircase that was right in front of my face built into that cliff. After reading Change Your Questions, Change Your Life by Marilee Adams for the first time, I realized I had been going about everything all wrong. I'm not certain the exact moment that it clicked for me, but it was somewhere deep within the pages of her book. I had dutifully been blindly following all the quaint quotes (as you'll learn, I love a good quote!) that everyone knows. From the obvious "don't put all your eggs in one basket" to "always have a plan B". Sometimes this process worked out, but not nearly often enough to claim success was a simple pattern. While some will get lucky and succeed the first time, some painfully slowly, and some from plainly just being too dumb to quit, I want to show you the simple way to reach every goal in your head. And the goals you don't know you have yet. Simple but not easy. Easy would be nice, wouldn't it? I thought for much of my early adulthood that I could find a way to make anything "easy", as I had done up until then. As you know, teenagers know everything there is to know about life, and I was no exception. As it would turn out, the only thing with an "easy button" is Staples. After roughly fifty-eleven hard-won lessons, I have come to realize that success is just a defined decision we make.

Along the way I also realized that commitment to your goal is a critical part of success. In that moment I became a "Basket Case". I have heard my entire life all the cliches that are meant to sound positive yet are actually perpetuating limiting beliefs. Things like "don't keep your eggs in one basket", "always have a plan B", "Don't jump in head first", and "Just dip your toe in" may sound like good advice on the surface but in reality they are all differing ways to let fear rule you. I wholeheartedly disagree with this notion. If you are willing to put in the work to prepare for the journey to success, you can conquer and goal. This book is my attempt to give you the framework to run face first into the life of your dreams. My goal is to show you why you absolutely should put all of your eggs in one basket. You must commit to your goals fully. Once you achieve the current goal, grab a new basket for your next goal and start filling that one. Rinse. Repeat.

You have probably heard Henry Ford's quote, "Whether you think you can or think you can't, you're right.". He was correct. I will even take it a step further by saying that I KNOW you can reach your version of success if you follow the steps in this book. You will learn how to choose success daily. You will see just how many times you have a choice to make and how to make it better. Making these improved decisions requires work, perseverance, courage, tenacity, introspection, and occasionally some good old-fashioned stubbornness. You do have it in you to accomplish your wildest dreams.

Reaching your goals is just a process. There are several steps to the process, but the procedure is exactly the same for each goal. The key is doing each and every step and doing them in order. There are no shortcuts to success. My ADHD likes to tell me that I should be able to skip the first few steps or at least the "easy" steps. I must remind myself more often than not, that the most important steps are in laying the groundwork. Building a solid foundation isn't necessarily the most fun or shiny part of the process, but it is a crucial step in the process. You cannot build a skyscraper from the top down.

Many people, myself included, will minimize the successes and maximize the failures in their lives. They will minimize successes in the name of being humble. That is rarely the case. In actuality, it is often out of fear of ridicule or shame that others won't approve of their decisions or goals. Some people also will downplay their accomplishments because they feel it is inauthentic to celebrate each step of achievement or because some part of the process wasn't executed with perfection. Often it is easy to forget that we deserve to honor the work we have put in without the lens of comparison to those we perceive as being ahead of us in some arbitrary way.

On the opposite end of the spectrum, people will also maximize their perceived failures, or potential failures, as a form of self-preservation. They are so afraid of failing that they think one failure means they will fail at everything. It doesn't even have to be a "real" failure. You may forget to turn on your smartwatch to track a run. Instead of being happy that it was a great run, you perceive it as a failure because your watch didn't know about it. Can you think of anything that you have tricked yourself into seeing as a failure? Other times, it is a fear of success itself that hinders us. We will imagine that the success will increase the pressure we feel to perform for an audience that may or may not be watching our every move. I struggle with this feeling now and again. When I catch myself living small for others, I remind myself that I'm only the main character in MY life. Unless you're being followed by TMZ, those around you probably don't notice as much about what you're up to as you might imagine. That's not to rain on your parade but rather to release the fear that may be holding you back. Go ahead and dance to your drum like no one is watching yet.

You will have far more success in life than otherwise. In fact, your success rate for waking up daily is at 100% so far! You are already doing a great job! Remember that when working toward success in your goals, you will, at times, have a failure. Fail is not the F word that society pretends it to be. No matter how big the failure is or how devastating the loss feels in the moment... failure will always, no matter what, feel better than regret. Failure feels better than regret every damn time. Keep working toward your successes after you fail. If you sense any doubt in your ability to succeed, doubt the doubt. Failing is only a step on your path. It is part of the path. You put in the work. If you succeed on the first try, great! If you fail at anything along the way, learn from it and fail forward. Write it down. See where the problem was and try again. Turn it into growth. Take the opportunity to learn for granted by the lived experience. If you must fail again, fail bigger and better than you did before, and learn more than the last time as well. Do not let the fear of failure keep you paralyzed at the starting line. Like Michael Jordan said, "I can accept failure. Everyone fails at something. But I can't accept not trying.". I say "It's ok to be afraid. It's not ok to let it stop you." every chance I get. Let the fear lead you. Whenever you feel afraid of doing something, that is the thing you need to do next. Fear is literally telling you, "This is the way". Follow your fear all the way to your wildest dreams. Fear rarely looks like screaming and running away, arms flailing around you. It more often looks like avoidance of a task or "forgetting" something that needs to be done. Do the thing. Face the fear. You'll probably realize it wasn't THAT bad.

Comparing ourselves to others is another activity that can stop us in our tracks. There is also nothing good that comes from looking at the paths of others. It is easy to compare yourself to someone else on a similar path and become disenchanted. You cannot compare your beginning to another person's accomplishment. This is setting yourself up for failure. We don't do that here. Something I have learned over my years living in SoCal is nothing, and I mean NOTHING, started the way you are served it. There are so many tricks of the camera and help from others that you can never see from the outside. The world is a stage. And there are a million stagehands out there. There are green screens and filters and Photoshop and editing and AI and entire teams of people supporting that "self-made" person. We all need help throughout many steps as we strive for our goals and that is ok!

Your goals, obstacles, resources; your entire journey is just that. YOUR journey. Not that of your neighbors or the nay-sayers that sneak into your life. I believe my friend Denise said it best when she said, "Just because we can see each other doesn't mean we're on the same road.". This hit hard. Comparisons are deadly to your dreams. Whenever you catch yourself beating yourself up for not being the first or quite as far along on your journey as another, remind yourself that those are your peers. They are only proof that success in your venture is obviously a possibility.

You are your only competition. You only need to be better than you were yesterday, even if no one else can see your growth yet. Some growth is internal. Don't forget that. Look at flowers. Blooming is just one step of their journey. They begin as seeds hidden underground. They grow their roots first. Then, they reach through the pressure of the world on their backs to sprout. They reach toward the sky, silently working toward the day they will bloom brilliantly. Their success is inescapable. You, too, will bloom. Again and again. Season after season.

Your success is not only possible but inevitable if you follow the guidelines of the Basket Case method described within these pages. You must start by knowing who you are and what motivates you; clearly define your one goal; chart the path that it takes to reach your specific goal in great detail; take at least one of the steps on your map daily; and repeat. That's it. Simple, right? If you follow the steps in this book, you will reach your goals, whether your goal is to have a million dollars or you are starting with a million dollars. You will cross your finish line.

CHAPTER 2 – GETTING TO KNOW YOU

You have likely heard it said, "To get where you are going, you must first know where you are". Obviously, this is useful literally and metaphorically. You will start mapping your path by first calibrating your internal compass and defining where you are. This may be the most important step as it helps define the path you take to move forward on every goal you have now and for goals to come.

If you have ever watched Alice in Wonderland, you know the frustration that can be caused by being asked, "Who are you?". Most especially when the person asking is the person in the mirror. I wish I could tell you that all you need to do is eat a sweet biscuit and have a cup of tea to know yourself better. Unfortunately, there is no getting around this step. Impending frustration or not, you need to ask yourself, "Who am I?". Many philosophers and theologians alike call upon us to look within ourselves. In this section, you will probably have some growing pains. We all have many masks (especially if you are neurodivergent like me) we wear with different people and in different places. Even with ourselves. The idea is to remove the masks, most of all, the ones you wear in the mirror. Seeing *all* of yourself, including the parts that you do not want to face, or admit to, will assist you exponentially in the future. Understanding yourself as a whole, full being will allow you to capitalize on your strengths to the fullest and exercise areas of weakness in more productive ways.

It took me years of trying, untold hours in therapy, and a couple of new and improved diagnoses to discover who I am today. In truth, I am still reflecting and learning. Learning about my ADHD and autism has gifted me with a new, clearer hindsight. I am now able to view certain "flaws" I thought I had as neurodivergent traits. I better understand why I struggled with things society told me were easy my whole life. This insight is great to have now as I am learning techniques and life hacks to manage my symptoms in less personally destructive ways. If I'm honest, sometimes this knowledge pisses me off that I wasn't diagnosed earlier. I am a freaking poster child for ADHD and autism in an AFAB person.

Having the knowledge when I was a child would have given me the tools and language to protect and advocate for myself. Unfortunately, the world just did not have an understanding of neurodiversity when I was a child. I try to give myself the grace to accept that help was not possible for me then and to use my voice to advocate for more to be done for the next generation with the same struggles to be better supported earlier. The best way to pass on the knowledge is to encourage as many people as possible to dive into themselves. Understanding who you are and how your mind works, whether you are neurotypical or neurodivergent, is the first step to finding success in your life.

One way to better know yourself is by taking a personality test. A personality test is a great place to start because they are easy to access and are guided. Often, we don't focus any of our time on introspection. The avoidance of observing our own mental processes may simply be because we don't know where or how to start. In this chapter, I've put together a few (mostly free) ways to learn about and begin your journey to self-knowledge. Please take at least one assessment. You will also need time to reflect on the new insight you have into yourself once you have taken the test. Take time to see yourself for who you truly are. See your strengths and weaknesses. See yourself as a whole being. Look into your shadows and find the incredible, multifaceted person you are.

Myers-Briggs Type Indicator

Probably the most well-known test is the Myers-Briggs Type Indicator (MBTI). Many employers, agencies, and college guidance counselors use it to get some insight about how you tick. The CIA uses this personality assessment. Regardless of your or my opinion of the CIA, I bet we can agree that they know what they are doing when it comes to understanding how people work. That is why it is the first assessment I bring up.

There are several free versions of this test you can take online. As well as the original that can be taken for a fee. This test was created in 1944 by the mother/daughter team of Katherine Cook Briggs and Isabel Briggs Myers. This personality typology is given to categorize everyone into one of sixteen possible personality types. You may take this test for a small fee and read more in-depth about your type at www.myersbriggs.org. A similar test that is free is at www.16personalities.com.

Below I have listed very brief overviews of the 16 types of the Myers-Briggs Type Indicator.

An **ISTJ** is someone who tends to have a rational outlook on life. They are willful and reserved. They have a methodical drive and compose their actions carefully to carry them out with intense purpose. The ISTJ personality type is thought to be the most abundant type, making up roughly 13% of the total world population. Their defining characteristics are integrity, practical logic, and dedication to duty. This makes ISTJs a vital component to many families, as well as organizations that uphold traditions. Their strict adherence to rules and standards makes them a good fit in careers such as law offices, regulatory bodies, and the like.

An **ISFJ** is someone who tends to be steady, warm, and unassuming in their own way. They're efficient and responsible. They give careful attention to the details of their everyday lives. The ISFJ personality type is quite unique because many of their individual traits are defined by their overall personality type. ISFJs have excellent analytical abilities while still being sensitive. Though they are generally reserved, ISFJs are often receptive to change and new ideas. ISFJs are much more than the sum of their parts. It is the way they use their strengths that defines who they really are.

An **ISTP** is someone with an individualistic mindset. They do well pursuing goals without needing much external management. ISTPs love to explore with their hands and their eyes, touching and examining the world around them with cool rationalism and spirited curiosity. People with this personality type are natural-born makers, moving from project to project, building the useful and the superfluous for the fun of it. They learn from their environment as they go. Often mechanics and engineers, ISTPs find no greater joy than in getting their hands dirty pulling things apart, and putting them back together, just a little bit better than they were before. The ISTP explores ideas through creating, troubleshooting, and first-hand experience. They learn best through trial and error.

The **ISFP** personality tends toward having an open mind when approaching life and new experiences. They meet new people with grounded warmth. Their ability to stay in the moment helps them discover exciting opportunities. ISFP personalities are true artists, but not necessarily in the typical sense. Rather, it's that they use aesthetics and design and even their actions to push the limits of social norms. ISFPs enjoy upsetting traditional expectations with experiments in beauty and behavior. They definitely have a punk side.

INFJs tend to approach life with deep thoughtfulness and imagination. Their inner vision, personal values, and principled version of humanism guide them in all areas of life. Although INFJs are thought to be the rarest personality type, they leave their mark on the world. They have a deep sense of integrity and idealism, yet they are not just dreamers. INFJs take concrete steps to realize their goals and make a lasting impact on their environment.

INFJs have a unique combination of personality traits that make them complex and very versatile. For example, INFJs can speak with great conviction, especially when standing up for their own ideals. At other times, they may choose to be soft-spoken, preferring to keep the peace rather than challenge the ideals of others.

INFPs tend to be open-minded and imaginative. They apply a caring and creative approach to everything they set out to do. Although they may seem quiet or unassuming, INFPs have vibrant and passionate inner lives. They can happily lose themselves in daydreams, inventing all sorts of stories in their minds. These personalities are known for their sensitivity. They feel called to help others and develop deep, meaningful relationships. INFPs may sometimes feel lonely or invisible, adrift in a world that doesn't seem to appreciate the traits that make them unique.

INTJs are thoughtful tacticians who love perfecting the details of life. They apply creativity and rationality to everything they do. Their inner world is often a private, complex one. This personality type comes with a very strong independent streak. INTJs don't mind acting alone, perhaps because they don't like waiting around for others to catch up with them. They also generally feel comfortable making decisions without asking for anyone else's input or permission. At times, this lone-wolf type of behavior can come across as insensitive, as it fails to take into consideration other people's thoughts, desires, and plans.

INTPs are often flexible thinkers who enjoy taking an unconventional approach to many aspects of life. INTPs will seek out unlikely paths; mixing willingness to experiment with their own personal creativity. INTPs pride themselves on their unique perspectives and high intellect. They often find themselves puzzling over the mysteries of the universe. This may explain why some of the most influential people of all time, like Albert Einstein, Marie Curie, Tina Fey, and Elliot Page have been INTPs. They aren't afraid to stand out in the crowd.

ESTPs tend to be energetic and action-oriented. They deftly navigate whatever is In front of them. They love discovering life's opportunities, whether socializing with others or in more personal pursuits. ESTPs always have an impact on their immediate surroundings. ESTP personalities love to be the center of attention They are entertaining with a blunt and earthy humor. ESTPs keep their conversation energetic, with a good dose of intelligence. They often leap before they look, fixing their mistakes as they go, in place of preparing contingencies and escape clauses while sitting idle.

ESFPs are people who love vibrant experiences, engage eagerly in life, and take pleasure in discovering the unknown. They can be very social, often encouraging others into shared activities. If anyone is to be found spontaneously breaking into song and dance, it is the ESFP personality type. They often get caught up in the excitement of the moment and want everyone else to feel that way, too. ENFPs are quite generous with their time and energy when encouraging others, and no other personality type does it with such charisma.

ESTJs possess great fortitude, emphatically following their own sensible judgment. They often serve as a stabilizing force among others and offer solid direction amid adversity. ESTJs are representatives of tradition and order. They use their understanding of what is right, wrong, and socially acceptable to bring their communities together. Embracing the values of honesty, dedication, and dignity, ESTJs are valued for their clear advice and guidance, making them great mentors. They happily lead the way on difficult paths. Taking pride in bringing people together, ESTJs often take on roles as community organizers. They work hard to bring everyone together in celebration of cherished local events or in defense of the traditional values that hold their communities together.

ESFJs are attentive and people focused. They enjoy taking part in their social community. Their achievements are guided by their willingness to offer guidance to others and decisive values. People who share this personality type are, for lack of a better word, popular. ESFJs enjoy supporting their friends and loved ones, organizing social gatherings, and doing their best to make sure everyone is enjoying themselves. They are social creatures and thrive on staying up to date with their friends. ESFJs are concerned with their appearance, their social status, and the standings of other people around them.

ENFPs are people who tend to embrace big ideas and actions that reflect their sense of hope and goodwill toward others. Their vibrant energy often flows in many directions. ENFPs are outgoing, openhearted, and open-minded. With their lively, upbeat approach to life, they stand out in any crowd. ENFPs don't just care about having a good time. This personality type runs deep, much like their longing for meaningful and emotional connections with other people.

ENFJs are warm, forthright types. They love helping others and tend to have strong ideas and values. ENFJs back their perspective with the creative energy to achieve their goals. ENFJs often feel called to serve a greater purpose in life. They are thoughtful and idealistic. ENFJs strive to have a positive impact on other people and the world around them. They rarely shy away from an opportunity to do the right thing, even if doing so isn't easy. They are born leaders, which explains why these personality types can be found among many notable coaches, politicians, and teachers. There are very few things that bring ENFJs a deeper sense of joy and fulfillment than guiding friends and clients to grow into the best version of themselves.

ENTPs tend to be bold and creative. They can deconstruct and then rebuild ideas with great mental agility. They pursue their goals vigorously despite any resistance they might encounter along the way. No one loves the process of mental sparring more than the ENTP personality type, as it gives them a chance to exercise their effortlessly quick wit, broad accumulated knowledge base, and capacity for connecting disparate ideas to prove their points. ENTPs enjoy playing devil's advocate. They don't always do this because they are trying to achieve some deeper purpose or strategic goal. Sometimes it's for the simple reason that they find fun in the debate.

ENTJs (me) are decisive people who love momentum and accomplishment. They gather information to construct their creative visions and rarely hesitate long before acting on them. ENTJs are natural leaders. People within this personality type embody the gifts of charisma and confidence. They project authority in a way that draws crowds together behind a common goal. However, ENTJs are also characterized by an often ruthless level of rationality. They often use their drive, determination, and sharp minds to achieve whatever end they've set for themselves.

Enneagram

The Enneagram is another personality typology. It uses nine personality types, just over half the number of types in the Myers-Briggs Type Indicator. I refer to the Enneagram most often with my coaching clients. I feel this typology dives a bit deeper for our purposes, though I do recommend knowing your type in both typologies before doing much introspection. Like above for the Myers-Briggs, here I list a brief synopsis of each enneagram type.

Ones are the Perfectionist of the Enneagram. They place a lot of emphasis on doing things correctly and following the rules. The Perfectionist can be extremely strict with themselves and others. They are rational yet idealistic. They tend to be principled, purposeful, self-controlled, and obviously perfectionistic. They're the types who love to carry around planners. They throw their weight behind a good cause. When it comes to spending time with friends and family, the perfectionist is intentional. A problem they often struggle with is they tend to focus on their perceived imperfections and rarely stop to smell the roses. It is often difficult for them to enjoy life if everything isn't exactly in order. They hate making mistakes, and others often describe them as judgmental or critical.

Twos are the Helpers. They want to be liked and find ways that they can be helpful to others. This type fears being unlovable and often seeks out ways to be part of the group. The Helper is the caring, interpersonal type. They tend to be demonstrative, generous, and often people-pleasing. The helper can also be a little possessive. They find value in being needed. To secure a feeling of value, they often want to help out and nurture those around them. Their big hearts make them a bit more sensitive than some of the other Enneagram types.

Threes are the Achiever of the enneagram. They want to be successful and admired by other people. They are hyper-conscious of their public image. Achievers fear not being seen as valuable, and therefore being a failure, by other people. You will recognize an Achiever by their adaptive, excelling, and driven nature. They are success-oriented and want to be the best. They have an easy charm and confidence with which they often inspire those around them.

Fours are the Individualist of the enneagram. They want to be unique and to experience deep, authentic emotions. Individualists fear they are flawed. They are overly focused on if and how they are different from other people. This type is sensitive, somewhat withdrawn, dramatic, and self-aware. However, they are also known for establishing deeper connections emotionally and creating beauty in their world.

Fives are the Investigator of the enneagram. Investigators seek knowledge and understanding. They are more comfortable with data than other people. Being overwhelmed by their own needs or the needs of other people is the Investigators' biggest fear. The Investigator is an intense, cerebral type. This type is always on the search for more knowledge. They relish their alone time. This makes them inherently innovative and curious creatures.

The Skeptics of the enneagram are the **sixes**. They are preoccupied with security, seek safety, and like to be prepared for any situation that may present itself. For Sixes, the greatest fear is being unprepared and unable to defend themselves and others from danger. The Skeptic is responsible and committed. They are security-oriented and want to be safe. Because of this, they are drawn to the safety of familiar and cozy things. They can be both suspicious and anxious, but they're also dependable, engaging, caring, and compassionate in life.

Sevens are the enneagrams' Enthusiast. They want to have as much fun and adventure as possible and can become bored easily. Enthusiasts fear experiencing emotional pain, especially sadness. Often, they actively seek to avoid it by staying busy. They're fun-loving and naturally spontaneous. The Enthusiast is the proverbial social butterfly. They can adapt to many different social circles and situations. They are optimistic but can also be distractible and scattered.

Eights (me) are the Challengers of the enneagram. Challengers seek to stand up for what they believe in. The greatest fear of the Challenger is to be powerless, so they focus on controlling their environment. They are natural-born leaders. Challengers are powerful, dominating types, but on the plus side, they're self-confident, empowering, loyal, and honorable. They stand up for the people they care about and the causes they believe in. They are willful and always take the initiative in any given situation. They are adaptable but also like to be in control. This can make them confrontational at times.

Nines are the Peacemakers. They like to go with the flow and let the people around them set the agenda. Peacemakers fear pushing people away by prioritizing their own needs, and they tend to be passive in nature. The Peacemaker is easygoing to the point of self-effacing. They are receptive, reassuring, agreeable, trusting, and non-judgmental. The Peacemaker is a great listener. They enjoy being at home and having stability. They should be listened to when offering advice to others. A potential downfall for this type is that they can grow complacent in their own lives.

Some other notable personality typologies are the Zodiacs, the Blood Type Personality Theory, the Big Five, DiSC, and the Keirsey Temperament Sorter. The latter is very similar to the Myers-Briggs Type Indicator in tests and groupings. I mention the first two because of their popularity if not necessarily their validity. The Blood Type Personality theory is still fairly popular in Japan. I'm type O-. The various Zodiacs of the world are fun to know, and many people swear by them. There may be a correlation between personality types and one's blood type or birth chart. I'll let you decide if these are areas of self-knowledge you want to subscribe to more in-depth. There is plenty of information both online and in many other books.

The point of the assessments is to better understand yourself on a deeper level. For me, learning about ADHD and ASD was also enlightening. It gave me clarity on areas of myself that I believe were flaws or areas that required suppression. Turns out I just needed to understand those parts of me to learn how to better work with my skills and accommodate my disabilities. I was able to recognize the symptoms of my neurodiversity because of how deeply was I diving into knowing myself.

If anyone close to you would be willing to take the tests along with you, it can be a good way to learn new ways of working with someone productively. I recommend learning the personality types of anyone with whom you will be working often or spending a great deal of time. Especially if you struggle to communicate well with them. There is something to be said for knowing the type of your partner or other family members and close friends. Having the added knowledge of each other may ease areas of conflict and create a deeper bond between you. As we are the sum of the 5 people we spend the most time with, knowing those closest to us can deepen our knowledge of self as well.

A final thought on understanding yourself, if at all possible, go to therapy. Thankfully, the importance of therapy has been becoming more widely accessible and socially acceptable. Many insurances are covering therapy now and there are more and more virtual options available. If your employer offers benefits, you may have a number of free therapy visits through your company's EAP benefit. Even if you feel happy and well-adjusted, consider therapy. Therapists are trained to dig into deeper levels of you than you may even realize exist at this time. A good therapist will help you better understand yourself, your needs, and your relationships. They will give you the tools to vocalize healthy boundaries and nurture important relationships in your life.

I cannot stress this point enough. Find a way to go to therapy. Look online for referrals and reviews of therapists that meet the demographic that you would be comfortable around. You can find therapists that are safe for race relations, genderqueer folx, religious or non-religious, and just about any subject that can breed trauma. Even if you don't feel like you need therapy, just having someone unbiased to walk you through the day-to-day crap can make your already lovely life a bit lighter too.

Once you have taken some time to reflect on who you are as a person, the next steps should feel a smidge easier to work through. Bring a notebook and pencil (with an eraser) because the next chapter is going to need a bit more emotional elbow grease. I was just getting your brain primed for coming exercises.

CHAPTER 3 – YOUR MISSION AND MORE

Now that you have a good idea of who you are, you will explicate what it is, exactly, that you stand for. In this chapter, you will create your code of ethics, core values, and personal mission statement. You may already be familiar with these concepts or even have them defined professionally. While your professional versions may be similar to what you are about to write, these will be specific to you instead of a company or cause. You are welcome to, but never have to, share these ideas with anyone else. However, if you are comfortable doing so, please share them with your trusted friends or family. I have found that sharing these ideas creates a great dialogue between friends. I, too, would love to read them. Yes, really. If you are comfortable, please contact me at www.shiftwithbunni.com.

When writing each of your core values, mission statement, and code of ethics, you will want to be as honest and specific as possible. I also encourage you to always keep a copy of all three with you. Print them out and put a copy everywhere. On the fridge. In the office. In your car. Your phone lock screen. Anywhere that will keep them top of mind. Doing so will allow you to reference them while making difficult decisions as they present themselves.

Your code of ethics, core values, and mission statement will likely grow with you on this journey. You will want to review and revise them at regular intervals. I recommend doing so more often in the beginning. A possible schedule is monthly for three months, then every three months for half the year, and finally biannually to annually. I found this schedule to work well because much of your development happens near the beginning of this process. It takes some time to live with integrity for you to refine your statements into the best version for each season of your life. There may never be a "final version" of them as they will grow with you throughout your life. If you not only know your first code of ethics will not be the last but also schedule the updates as a regular part of your journey, writing them out isn't as scary. I know that perfectionism is good at sabotaging very personal projects such as these. At least, it is for me.

I am sharing my current version of all three with you as an example of form, detail, and layout. If you're anything like me, writing anything for the first time is one of the most daunting tasks. I trust seeing my versions will assist in you putting pen to paper. You can write them however feels right for you. Do not feel obligated to make yours look exactly like mine. Actually, they shouldn't look exactly like mine. These are your personal statements. They should be as unique as you are.

I review mine and adjust them to fit my personal growth journey as needed. In the beginning, I updated them every 3 to 6 weeks and then every month. Now I don't need to tweak them as often. I still review them at least annually or before a big project. I recommend keeping a separate notebook, folder, or computer file for them and dating them. There will come a day when you will want to reflect on how far you have come. Having this tangible record and timeline will give you a great understanding of your own personal growth journey.

Code of Ethics

Your code of ethics is a guide of personal principles that help you live up to your own standards and with integrity. It explains the expectations you have set for yourself. Your code of ethics provides a framework for how you want to interact with others, friends, clients, and colleagues alike, positively and progressively. Your code of ethics should list your goals and provide an overall idea of who you want the future you to look and act like. You can refer to your code of ethics in trying times to help you decide how to move forward in a way that best reflects your integrity.

When you are writing your own Code of Ethics, you will want to start with five to ten statements that reflect how you expect yourself to behave at any given moment. You will want to address your responses to both positive and negative situations. Once you have these overall statements you can go back and define them a bit more in depth.

The following is my Code of Ethics. You can see that I have written it in the first person and present tense. This technique makes it more real in my mind and, therefore, easier to implement in the moment of action.

My Personal Code of Ethics:

- ***I am grateful and appreciative for every day of my life.*** *I recognize my privileges and position in life. I will give whenever possible and contribute to my communities with my time and treasure.*
- ***I will always uphold my beliefs.*** *I believe that all living beings are inherently deserving of dignity.*
- ***I will treat others as they wish to be treated.*** *I understand that while I do not immediately know each person's desires and preferences, I will interact with them from a base level of respect and adjust accordingly to their wishes for continued integrity.*
- ***I will live authentically by maintaining honesty and transparency in both my professional and personal lives.*** *I am dedicated to being forthcoming with information as it is needed in all my relationships. I am obligated by my moral compass to keep all promises and commitments, no matter how insignificant they may appear to me in the moment, even to myself.*
- ***I will hold myself accountable for my mistakes and shortcomings.*** *I strive for rarity in such situations yet will take responsibility for any harm that I cause and will work to right all wrongs.*
- ***I will continually strive for growth and improvement in myself.*** *I believe that living each day by my morals and virtues will encourage me to be the ethical, growth-minded person that I strive to be.*

Now that you have an idea of what a code of ethics looks like break out your handy dandy notebook and spend a few minutes outlining yours. Set a timer for ten minutes and just write down a dozen-ish "I statements" that relate to who you want to be and how you want to live. Don't worry about grammar or repetition of any themes at this moment. Just worry about getting the words on the paper. After you finish this chapter, return to your notebook and organize these thoughts. You can filter out anything that was repeated and potentially combine ideals that are separate but similar.

Core values

Core values are 3 to 5 value words or phrases that define who you are at your most basal. In other words, no matter the situation, if you act with these core values in mind, you will live up to your personal Code of Ethics every time. Let me say that again. No matter what the situation is, you will live up to your personal standards every time if you lean into these few phrases. Your core values are just that. Your CORE. These are the few words that shake you all the way to your bones. These are the words that your backbone is made of. These are the words that keep you standing tall even when your voice shakes. Your core values should move you every time you speak them. You want these to be motivational to you specifically and in any situation, good or bad. They will also grow and evolve with you as you stretch yourself as a person. You will want to review these words often, not only to ensure that you are living up to them but also to make certain they are the core values that are apropos to your current seat at the table of life.

My current three core values are as follows:

>   ***Intention-*** *I am intentionally full of gratitude for my life; the successes and the struggles. I am aware of my intention with every decision I make.*

>   ***Growth mindset-*** *I strive to be fit and healthy; both physically and emotionally. I am determined to learn and grow each day. I am better today than I was yesterday. I am my only competition.*

>   ***Service to others-*** *I provide service to those around me to the best of my abilities. I lift them up with my words, actions, time, and treasure. I raise my voice for those who haven't the strength. I invite everyone to my table. I radiate the belief that we are stronger together and living fuller when leaning into the wisdom of those different than us.*

These have been my core values for several years now. I still revisit them annually to ensure that I am living authentically. As you can see in my example, I have written a power statement after each core value. These are "I" statements that help me align my thoughts consciously to live up to my personal values.

Now it is your turn to define your core values. Take a sheet of paper and set a timer for five minutes. I want you to time yourself for this exercise because it is easy to want to use all the value words to describe yourself, but we only want three. Start by just randomly writing value words that are important to you, such as family, security, connection, creativity; all over the page. Fill up the page. Write as many as you can think of in your allotted five minutes.

Second, spend a few minutes grouping the words with similar definitions or that are encompassed within another word. An example would be caring and thoughtful could both fit into compassionate.

Now that you have only words with different meanings set a timer for one minute. This time you will cross off any words that you could live without. One of the most difficult parts of this exercise is striking words that we know are important. Try to keep in mind that these are not your ONLY values, but instead only your most important values at this time in your life. As you narrow your list, remember that if everything is special, nothing is special.

Finally, set a timer for ten seconds. Use this time to circle the three to five words of the words that are left that you cannot live without. These are your first core values. On a new sheet of paper, write each value giving yourself several lines between each. Next, write your power statements in this space. In the beginning, I recommend reviewing and refining these statements weekly for one month. Then once monthly. After three months, or so, you should have a solid list of core values and accompanying power statements. At this point, you can review them less often. Try setting a reminder to review once or twice a year now.

Mission Statement

A personal mission statement is, again, going to be similar to what you would expect to see framed in an office building. The biggest difference is, of course, this one is personal. Your mission statement is a formal summary of your aims and values. To write your mission statement, review your current code of ethics and core values. You want to encompass both within one to three sentences. This may take several rounds of edits to accomplish a few fluid and authentic sentences.

My personal mission statement is as follows: **"It is my personal mission to live gently by seeking the positive in all things, to facilitate growth; to hold space for and honor the value of all others; to give to my communities in time and treasure; and to use my knowledge and dedication to excellence to lift others into their own light."**.

You may also want to review other sample mission statements online to get an idea of how you want yours to go. Just like with your personal code of ethics and core values, your mission statement will grow with you. You will also need to review and refine it over the coming weeks and months until you reach a personal mission statement that only needs annual or semiannual review.

Once you are satisfied with your statement, print it out. Put a copy in your wallet, on your refrigerator, in the car, and on your desk. Take a picture with your phone and make it your lock screen. I know I sound like a broken record at this point, but this is important. I have mine framed on my desk, right next to my computer screen. You want to have it where you can see it regularly. This will aid in memorizing it and allow you to live up to your own standards more easily in any situation.

How does it feel to have written your code of ethics, core values, and mission statement? Do you feel more grounded? More secure in your self-identity? Perhaps you feel like you're living more authentically now that you have the words to explain yourself written down. You will find in later chapters that these statements of self will assist in preventing decision fatigue. Using them regularly will prepare you for the difficult days to come as you endeavor to reach your goals.

CHAPTER 4 – WHERE YOU ARE?

Now that you know who you are, you need to know where you are. What are your goals? Which one are you working on right now? How do you decide? You most likely have many goals you would like to accomplish *someday*. There are goals in your life that you think would be nice to work on when you're "ready". The problem with this way of thinking is that you will never be ready. The timing will never be perfect. There will always be an excuse not to go for it if you allow for the excuse. The idea is to take the leap of faith and see how close to ready you actually already are.

In this chapter, you will determine what the starting line is. You will do this by writing out a master list of all your goals for "someday". You will use this list to create your map to success. These map coordinates will not only vary a great deal from person to person but also from goal to goal. Despite all the potential differences in the details, the steps to draw your map will be the same for every single goal you wish to achieve. Odds are, if you are reading this book, you began reading it with a goal in mind. But what if you aren't certain of what your goal is? That's ok, too.

First, you will write out your "bucket list" of all the goals you would like to achieve by *one of these days*. Write them all down. All of them. From the wildly huge to the teeny tiny goals. There will be different seasons in your life. They will each require different types of goals. Write down the outlandish and crazy goals. The impossible goals. The so-easy-you-should-have-done-them-already goals. And everything in between. Don't worry about what anyone else might think about your goals. Frankly, you need not show the list to anyone, so go big with it. This is your list, and if you want to skydive dressed like Sailor Moon for your 50th birthday, then it belongs on this list! I mean it! Write down everything you want to accomplish in this life.

If you struggle to think of goals, or if the grumpy old Negative Nancy who lives in the apartment above your brain just will not shut up long enough for you to make the list, imagine yourself in a decade. Who will you be after to kick Nancy out? Who are you then? What do you do? Where do you work? What clothes do you wear? How is your hair styled? Do you live alone or with someone? Do you have pets, kids, or plants? Where do you live? What do you eat? How is your health? How do you relax and treat yourself? What kind of friends do you have? Go into great detail. Write it in first person if you can. You can use the third person if that feels easier to begin with.

After you have the new you described, make 3 columns on a sheet of paper. Leave the middle column blank for right now. Write every way you listed your dream self on one side. Write how you are now across from each version of your dream self. For example, if you said you have long hair in ten years, but you have short hair now. "I have short hair" goes in one column, while "I have long hair." goes in the other column. Your goal goes in the middle column. In this example, to get from short hair to long hair, your goal is to grow out your hair. Another example would be if you currently have a Prius but dream you drives a tricked-out four-door hardtop Jeep. Then your goal is to save for the Jeep.

Once you have all your goals on paper, it is time to organize them. Can you group any of them together by theme, location, or another key marker? Are any of them dependent on one another? Can any of the goals be combined? If you can combine some, you have instantly increased your productivity on those goals by 100%. Go you! After connecting the ones that are related, organize them into groupings of big, small, or dependent on other goals.

These goals will assist you in making a chronologically-ish ordered master bucket list of your goals. Keep in mind that the time frame for the big goals may be sort of nebulous. Don't feel like you must pick a specific date to complete your goals. We will discuss time frames later. The big goals should be goals that take a while to complete. The small goals take less than a year to complete. Put the goals that are dependent on each other next to each other on your lists. This is your master list. It's your key to deciding what goal to work on at this moment. Also, remember that this list is not set in stone. It can and will grow and evolve right along with you as you accomplish more and more of your goals.

Now that you have assembled a master list of your goals pick the one you want to accomplish first. If this is too daunting of a task, at first, pick the ten most important to you. Wait a day and really reflect on your feelings about these ten goals. Truly weigh them on your heart. Why do you want to do them first? Are they easier than something else and you just want to dip your toes into the Basket Case water? Are you afraid to reach for the bigger goals? Are they sentimental? Do they feel like completion would have a profound effect on your future? Think deeply about what it is regarding these goals in particular that calls to you and come back to your list in a day or two.

After you have had some time contemplating their importance, cut your list in half. You want these to be the 5 goals that you couldn't live without. Take your time to reflect on which of the 5 goals left is the one you want the most right now. Which goal is calling to you? If you had to pick one goal and give up all the rest, which one would it be? There is always that one goal that you want most. Everyone has that one goal that would mean serious business to achieve. The one goal that would change the way we look at the universe.

I have experienced the consciousness shift that accompanies the achievement of a big goal a few times now. Something you should know about me is that I can do all things in spite, which strengthens me. Once upon a time, my then-husband told me that I couldn't afford to leave him and that I would never make more than him. I make well over double his income now, and I'm not stopping any time soon. Reaching that goal of surpassing his arrogance gifted me with the knowledge of my ability to reach higher than I had ever considered possible. As Ari says, "Thank you. Next!". I am so grateful for the fire his hatred lit in me. It gave me the gumption to give myself higher expectations for myself. I am no longer afraid to set impossible goals. Previously, I had believed that I didn't deserve more money. I doubted my worth because I wasn't formally educated. I dropped out of high school after ninth grade. And subsequently dropped out of community college a couple of times too. I had the limiting belief that that meant I would forever be living in poverty. I believed that I was only worthy of the peanuts I was making then. I believed that only rich folx made 6 plus figures. His disrespect ignited in me the audacity to believe I could be more. Look at me now. I went from living in a vehicle with my daughter, terrified of what could go wrong next, to thriving and living my dreams. The key is designing a plan that suits your dreams.

Which goal have you decided is the one? This is your first goal to achieve with the Basket Case method. Save your master list somewhere safe. You will want to be able to refer to it when you need to add a new goal and/or when it is time to mark a goal as completed. I recommend marking them with the date of completion as a way to see how far you have come. Keeping the master bucket list gives you a tangible record and timeline of how far you have come and shows you what you are in store for, as well as, what you are capable of. It can be extremely motivating to see the progress you have made on goals you thought you might never reach. Every day is a step closer to the "someday" of your dreams.

Next, you must elucidate what success means for you. There are many versions and levels of success. No one will have the same version. Everyone sees their summit differently. Even if you have the same goal as someone else, your successes could look completely different. For instance, if you and your friend both want to write a book, to your friend, just writing the book to completion could be success to them, while your version of success is not only the writing but also publishing and selling 100,000 or more copies. Reaching either summit will take different goalposts. Even though, when asked what your goal is, both of you may answer with the same response, "My goal is to write a book.". However, the result, or your versions of success, is not identical.

You will have a different definition of success for every goal. You will need to examine your goal and what completion of it looks like. Imagine every detail of reaching this goal. How do you feel? How will you celebrate? Who do you tell about your accomplishments? Are you a graduate? A business owner? A marathoner? A millionaire? Maybe you're a parent or a pianist. Each goal will come with its own success. Get as particular about defining your outcome as possible. You want to visualize what success means in full color. The completion of each goal will get you a step closer to a full and successful life. The more detailed you can make this picture, the easier it will become to see yourself reaching your goals. You will begin to believe that you are capable and deserving of reaching your dreams. Believing in yourself will help you reach your goals more reliably.

Defining the nitty gritty details of what success means to you with each goal is the catalyst to the accomplishment of the chosen goal. Scientists have found that the brain lights up the same areas when you visualize a thing or action as if you actually physically performed the task. This basically means that you can practice reaching your goals by visualizing achieving them. In the next section, you will learn techniques to improve visualization and more as you strive to bring your dreams to fruition.

CHAPTER 5 - RESOURCES

Resources are a staple for your success in every aspect of life. They are the well from which you will draw the strength, knowledge, and support necessary to reach your dreams. Imagine them as the tools in your tool belt for life. Depending on the job you are doing, you may use a single tool or any combination of these tools to complete the job. It is no different than when working toward your goals. Some of the resources that will have a big impact on the successful completion of your goals are a visualization board, mentors, the internet, libraries, and the people who will support you and to whom you can delegate tasks.

This section will hone in on each of these resources, specifically to give you ideas for using every tool available to the best of your accessible ability. Yes, your accessible ability. You don't have to have all the answers if you know someone else who knows what they are doing, too. You can do whatever it is that you need to be done if you can personally do it or if you know someone or something that can do it for you. You do not need to know how to do everything in order to reach your dreams. "Do what you can do well, hire what you can't do well.". If you think you cannot afford it, trade or barter for the service. Or use a free app or AI to get closer. You have some kind of access to everything you need. Maybe you have heard of the 5 degrees of separation. If so, then you already know that if you reach out far enough, you can find the answer to all of your needs.

I like to think of it much like what a general contractor does when building something. They can physically do almost anything on the job site, but they know when it is more beneficial and cost-effective to have someone who specializes in an area do that part of the job. For instance, when my grandfather would build an addition to a home, he had the experience to know what codes applied in each situation. He knew when it was more cost-effective to have a subcontractor come build a block wall because they would get it done promptly, and he was free to coordinate the rest of the build. He knew how to build the block wall, but he felt as though paying someone else to do it would be more advantageous to him physically doing it.

The same goes for reaching your goals. Perhaps your goal is to start a bee farm. You know everything there is to know about raising and tending to the bees. You know how to keep the drones and queen and everyone else happy and healthy, but you know nothing about getting the grant to cover the cost of material for a few new hives. It would behoove you to reach out to the people you know or to hire a professional grant writer instead of attempting to write the grant yourself. Or maybe you are a great salesperson for nutritious foods, but you know nothing about raising bees. If you want to sell honey, you will want to find someone who knows more about caring for bees. Maybe you are running an online clothing business but have trouble with numbers because you are afflicted with dyscalculia. You would want to have the help of someone who is a numbers whiz kid.

The point is that we aren't all great at everything. We don't know all there is to know about every given subject. Can we do most, if not all, of the mile markers on our lists? Probably. Will it be the most time and cost-effective way to move forward in your endeavors? Probably not. It takes a village to raise a baby and to reach a goal. No one is entirely self-made. We all could use some assistance to reach our dreams efficiently. This is not to say that you cannot do it all yourself. Just be prepared for more hands-on and time-consuming work, at least until you are willing to receive the help. And honestly, be ready for more headaches. There will inevitably be tasks that you avoid because you despise doing them, or times you mess up something because you just don't quite fully grasp how it works. Maybe you loathe the thought of filing your receipts and end up pulling out your eyelashes one by one come tax season because you just threw all the receipts into a plastic grocery bag, and now you are forced to sort the entire year of receipts all at once. Or perhaps you like staying up past your bedtime, so it's more difficult to wake up in time to get in your training runs before work, and now you only have 3 weeks before the 5k you signed up for to raise money for your child's school trip. Learning when and what to ask for help with is going to be a make-or-break skill on your way to achieving your goals.

These next few chapters dive a bit deeper into some common resources you may find helpful in your new tool belt. Use these tools as often as possible to make the best of your goals.

CHAPTER 6 - VISION BOARDS

The first tool that I want to talk about is the vision board. A vision board is a collection of motivating images that inspire you to continue an action. It can be physical or digital in today's age. Imagine a poster board with cutout pictures and power words or phrases mod-podged all over it. Or a wallpaper on your computer screen of a Canva collage page showcasing images that get you excited to work on your goals. The idea is that every time you see the vision board you will then visualize reaching the goals expressed on it. It is a blatant reminder that you are working toward a goal. You see, the brain is a funny creature. It cannot differentiate between what is real and imaginary. As I have mentioned before, when you imagine running a 5k from the starting line through the finish line and the subsequent celebration, your brain expresses the same electrical show as if you physically ran the race. The brain believes the vision to be true. This builds the neuropathways in your brain that lead to the completion of the goal. The more you visualize something as though it has already occurred, the more the RAS, the reticular activating system, is looking for a way to make it true. Your brain wants you to succeed. Use a vision board to get out of your own way and back on the road to success.

You can make a physical or virtual vision board, or you can do both. I prefer the physical version. I keep mine hung next to my dry-erase board, where I can see it first thing in the mornings. My daughter, however, prefers virtual and has hers as the lock screen on her phone. We make them together every year on New Year's Day. It's a fun bonding moment that we can still do now that she's a big kid with her own place.

Keep the vision board in front of you as much as possible. Your lock screen, office wall, closet door, next to the coffee pot, or wherever you look several times a day is a great way to make sure you see the board multiple times a day. You want to keep your goals top of mind. Maybe you will find that having both a physical and a digital copy of your visualization board is what works best for you. There is no wrong way of using your boards as long as you are using them. I encourage my clients to make one for every goal individually and one around New Year's or their birthday. I love the visualization board as a tool. It truly lets you live in the big picture. The visualization board is a great habit to start building your consistency of effort and provides an easy way to recall your purpose.

For a physical board, I save every print magazine, catalog, or arguably fun-looking flyer that I receive. This ensures that I have plenty of pieces that reflect my current core values, goals, and aesthetic for every board. If a virtual board sounds more like you, I recommend using Canva or Pinterest to make your own virtual visualization board. Both these sites offer easy and free customization options.

The reason the visualization board is such a powerful tool is that you are giving your reticular activating system (RAS) a specific idea of what to look for in the background. The RAS is a part of the brain that is constantly looking for new patterns that tell it you are moving in the correct direction. Have you heard the phrase "Seek and ye shall find"? Your RAS went full tilt when it heard that phrase. The RAS is constantly looking for and finding what you are seeking. Be aware of what you are telling your RAS to find. If you send it on a mission to find problems in the world, you will learn of problems you didn't know you had. On the other side of that coin, if you seek solutions to obstacles along your way, you will magically find the right way to fix the issues as they arise. Follow your RAS. Another area of the brain that may be assisting in our achievements is the mirror neuron. Mirror neurons are simply a type of brain cell that react if an action is performed or observed. A more in-depth definition is above my pay grade at the time being. But don't worry, YouTube University offers more information on the subject. (Thanks, Hank!) Mirror neurons are curious little things that may hold the secrets to why visualization is so effective when it comes to reaching a goal.

Pay special attention to the things your brain shows you on repeat. Notice when you see the same thing over and over and over again. These are areas where you will have the most growth. For instance, if you keep seeing a title or article subject, you should listen to your brain and read the book or article. Or, if you keep thinking of a certain person, give them a call to see if you can have coffee together and discuss what you both have been working on. Maybe they can help or know someone they can connect you with. Between the RAS and mirror neurons, we may know way more than we think we do. Science is working on the "how and why" they do their things. The trick is listening to our own

Jiminy Cricket in the meantime. Notice your environment and trust your intuition in the breaks between the more tangible steps in your journey to see the biggest results. The universe speaks louder when you listen.

CHAPTER 7 – YOUR MENTORS

The next tool in your tool belt is having a mentor. A mentor is someone who acts as an advisor to a less experienced person, who is referred to as their mentee. They are an experienced and trusted advisor who voluntarily agrees to help their mentee develop skills and competencies or reach a goal. Mentorships can be built through networking in professional or personal connections.

I will go as far as to say that you actually need two of them. One older and one younger than you are. Seek out at least a ten-year age difference if you can. You want mentors who can give you a different perspective than you have yourself. You're looking for guidance from a perspective that is far outside of your realm. Consider a mentor with whom you have a difference of age, gender, race, religion, or favorite ball team. To obtain the most development, you want the most robust and well-rounded influence available.

Most people have someone older than them that they look up to, if only in an informal way. However, those same people are often taken aback by the idea of a younger mentor. I swear by having both.

An older mentor is maybe an old family friend or elder work colleague. Maybe someone from your book club or a neighbor. You can even hire a mentor. They can be great at helping you see the bigger picture as well as giving unparalleled advice that only comes from longevity and lived experience. They tend to be consistent, and they can hear when you are lying to yourself. I'm fairly certain that it's a superpower you are given at a certain mental age. An elder mentor can call you out without being cruel while pulling the blinders off so you can see more of your path.

A younger mentor, however, can keep up to date with the tea. A younger mentor is a whole-ass mood. They can help keep your thoughts and ideas, and possibly your TikTok dance moves, fresh. They understand social trends and the relevant technology. They will low-key help you flex on the gram and make sure you never miss a snap streak. Younger mentors will program your proverbial VCR, fam. When looking for a youthful mentor, the younger the adult the more rizz. You want someone who can teach you how to use the latest technology, keep you hip to the newest music, and educate you on using the current slang correctly so you don't say something like "hip" when it's clearly cringe AF. Both aspects of mentorship are imperative to growth in today's world.

Having both types of mentors gives you an edge that someone trying to figure everything out the hard way doesn't have. Mentors share valuable life lessons. They can educate you on what to do and, when appropriate, what not to do as you work toward your goals. Mentors can advise on building, maintaining, or ending a relationship well. Romantic, platonic, professional, or otherwise. They can also introduce you to new relationships and help you make mutually beneficial connections to reach your goals. Mentors can inspire you to take the next step on your way to success, and hopefully, they can help keep you focused on the task at hand.

A good mentor encourages and enables your personal and professional development. They are masters at giving feedback that keeps you learning and reflecting on your own personal growth journey. Your mentor serves as a source of knowledge and support on your journey. They offer encouragement. They can help you set goals that are attainable and show you ways to traverse the path to success in the goals you set. Another trait a mentor offers is accountability. You are more likely to do what you say you are going to do if you know you must report back to your mentor with your progress. Your mentor is your best ally. They serve as someone willing to listen to your concerns and questions while giving valuable and constructive feedback so that you may grow from the experience with them. Mentors are not cheerleaders, though. While they will constructively encourage you, they do not blindly sponsor all your ideas.

Having a good mentor also sets you up for the day that you become a mentor. Becoming a mentor may be something you are consciously working toward, or it may come to be more organically. Have you ever heard "By your pupils, you'll be taught."? This is true for the mentor and mentee relationship as well. You will inevitably learn from those who you are mentoring as well. You will become more skilled at offering advice the more questions your mentees have. This will strengthen your own knowledge of what you are teaching as well as develop your interpersonal communication skills. You will better learn how to express yourself to different types of people during every mentorship. Much like the mentee benefits from having you introduce them to people who may make all the difference in their lives, you too will gain connections through your mentee.

When done right, mentorships are productive for both parties. The mentor and mentee gain knowledge and connections from the symbiotic relationship.

CHAPTER 8 - A COLLAGE OF OTHER RESOURCES

You have many resources available to you. Some examples are experts in the field, the worldwide interwebs, local classes, ChatGPT, habit trackers, the library, and more. Many of these resources are free or can be accessed for a small fee. You want to use as many resources as you can while reaching for your goals. Keep in mind that you do not need to reinvent the wheel. The good news is that most struggles that you will have, someone else has already had. And they posted a YouTube video on how to overcome this particular struggle in great detail. Use these resources to find a solution faster than chiseling out the answer the hard way.

The internet offers infinite possibilities of sources for knowledge. As mentioned earlier, www.myersbriggs.org, www.16personalities.com/tools, and www.enneagram.com are great sources of info on your personality test results, as well as, how you relate to all the other personalities out there. You can use this knowledge to enhance your understanding of the relationships that you already have or to see what relationship is missing from your life. Many articles in online media sources can give you insight or motivation along the way.

You can use Google, Bing, Duck Duck Go, or any other search engine of your choosing to find a relevant answer to just about any question you have. There are many degrees or certifications you can receive 100% online. YouTube and WikiHow can teach you how to play a ukulele, work on cars, write a resume, cook anything, and everything in between. Nowadays, more and more things are becoming virtual than ever before. From telemedicine to Zoom dating, you can do almost anything online. Use this to your advantage anytime you have a question or want to make a connection. There are great ways to find and meet people with a common interest or with whom you can pick their brains when you are looking for an answer via social media. Even a mentor. There is literally an app for that. Or more accurately, there are thousands of apps for that.

You can take trainings or classes on a myriad of subjects. Many community colleges offer continuing education courses you can take without being degree-seeking and certificate programs for skills or trades. Often these types of classes are completed in a few weeks to a few months, and they tend to be offered at a lower fee than the courses for degree-seeking schedules. Some classes can even be found for free.

Another great resource is a habit tracker. It is a good way to easily get a big picture of the habits you have down and to see the ones that need work. I use a grid paper laid out as a landscape. I make a column of the habits I want to track and then color in each grid to the right for every day I finish strong. At the end of each month, I can clearly see which habits to focus on in the next month and which ones I have conquered. This also allows me to celebrate my victories weekly or monthly, depending on how difficult the habit is to adhere to. If you are more virtual, there are many habit tracker apps in the metaverse nowadays. Finding what works for you is the key. I want to add a quick note that for us neurospicy folx, the formation of a habit may take longer or never quite feel like you imagine it "should". We are wired differently. Do not beat yourself up because Olivia Grace made it look effortless, and you feel like it is still a struggle on day 782 of your "new habit." Some things are just more difficult for us because our brains process effort and reward differently.

The library is the real OG of resources. The library, the Original Google, is an excellent source for reference, recreation, and serendipity. Libraries have been around for thousands of years. Before the internet shrank the world, libraries held the knowledge of mankind. More and more people (like me! Hi!) are writing books than ever before in history. This is making our libraries an even more vital tool to utilize. In today's high-speed, instant gratification world, the local library is often overlooked. It is a shame that this is the case. The library offers you access to any book in the building, any book within their connections for book shares, meeting rooms, internet and computer access, and more for free. There are even libraries that offer power tools, fishing gear, and sewing machines if you are so inclined to borrow such things. Libraries are an incredible and too often overlooked asset to our communities. If you don't have the time to go to the library, many libraries offer delivery or mobile services. Or if you just prefer listening to your books, there's even an app for that. Libby is the library app. All you need is a current library card to set up an account, then you have access to thousands of audiobooks right on your phone or tablet for free.

Your library is also most likely home to various group or club meetings. If you are looking to network, you should check out the monthly meeting calendar. While you are at it, you may also find a book club of interest to you. I have included a list of the books that I have referenced in this writing or that I feel everyone seeking growth or self-improvement should read in the back of this book.

With the sudden rise in awareness of the existence of AI, there is a new hype around ChatGPT, Bing image creator, and the like. These are great life-hack resources as well. Honestly, most of us have been using various forms of AI for years, even though we may not have known it at the time. Siri, Google Assistant, and the chatbot that processed your refund for Amazon are all powered by AI. There are many areas of life that can be made easier or more efficient by AI. You can save lots of time by just speaking to your smartphone to set a reminder of your friend's birthday that repeats annually and gives you an alert a week in advance. You can also use a more specified AI to do other things that will take some of the weight off your shoulders. Need a headshot or resume and cover letter for the dream job that you just heard was hiring today? Want to design a workbook but don't know where to start? Need a better way to explain astrophysics to your 11-year-old niece who will not stop asking why? AI can create a new headshot of you, write a cover letter specifically for that company, design a sample outline for the workbook, and give you a script for astrophysics for adolescents in just seconds. Having a rough draft that you can tweak to fit your needs so quickly can take much of the situational stress off of you and give you the time and clarity to truly design the life you want and still have the time and energy to make dinner at a reasonable time. AI cannot solve all your problems yet, but it can definitely make many problems more manageable. Learning to utilize AI and these other tools and resources will improve your quality of life in a hurry.

CHAPTER 9 - THE PEOPLE AROUND YOU

Friends and family are like your personal cheer squad, ready to support you every step of the way. The people who care about you are a great resource. Think of that one friend or family member who always tells it like it is—ask them to be your sounding board as you navigate your goals. You'll want someone who can give you gentle yet honest feedback and, most importantly, someone you can trust with your dreams and vulnerabilities. Remember to be mindful of their time and feelings as well. You do not want to make them feel taken advantage of just because they are sort of built-in for you.

Speaking your goals out loud can feel daunting, especially before you've achieved success. It is also, unfortunately, common for adults to err on the side of caution. This is probably with good intentions that they will tell you not to do it or that it can't be done. Whenever I think about this reaction from people who we would consider to be on our side, I think of a dear friend. Her response to finding out that I was going to move shocked and angered me a bit, if I'm honest. I told her I was going to move to Minnesota to be with my ex. She reflexively asked, "What if it doesn't work out?". I replied with, "At least I got out of Missouri." but it hurt my feelings at the moment. I have reflected on that moment many times over the years. She was hurt that I was leaving and worried about me moving 14 hours away. She was trying to protect me. Even though her words were negative, her intention was loving. It can be difficult to separate the fear from the love for some. And that's ok but it won't sustain your goals. That's why having a supportive ally who can guide you realistically but not negatively toward your aspirations is so crucial. They're not just there to cheer you on during the good times (though that's important, too); they're there to help you push through challenges and stay focused on what matters most.

Delegation is another game-changer in your toolkit. It's about identifying tasks that either drain your energy or take up too much of your precious time. Maybe it's getting your family more involved in household chores or hiring someone to handle the nitty-gritty details that keep you from focusing on your passions. Consider those tasks that you dread or simply don't excel at, even if you enjoy them. For example, I love using Canva for creative projects, but I found that investing in pre-made templates saves me hours each month. It's a win-win: I get to unleash my creativity without the time sink, and I can use those saved hours to focus on more impactful work at home and in my businesses.

When evaluating how you spend your time, think about the areas where a little delegation could go a long way. Could assigning specific chores to your kids free up mental space for you to excel at work? Would sharing household responsibilities with your spouse give you the freedom to pursue your side hustle more effectively? Would ordering Hello Fresh allow you to eat more nutritious meals without spending precious time lost at Ralph's? It's all about finding balance and maximizing productivity without losing sight of what's truly important at the end of the day. Quality time should always be the priority. Our lives are too short to not enjoy as much as possible.

And don't forget the power of bartering! You can have a lot of fun with this one. Especially if you get creative. If you have a neighbor with skills that complement yours—say they're a CPA and you're a dog lover—why not trade services? You can walk their dog on your days off in trade for them doing your taxes. Or if your best friend's mom loves to cook but needs help mowing the yard and taking out the trash, maybe you and your friend can go over on Thursday nights to have a nice home-cooked meal dinner with Mom. While she packs you half a week's leftovers, you can mow before you head home. It's a practical way to support each other's goals while making the most of your time and talents. And more importantly, it strengthens your community.

Remember, asking for help isn't just about getting things done—it's about building relationships based on mutual respect and support. Whether you're offering a hand or reaching out for assistance, do it with grace and appreciation. Your time is valuable, and so are the connections you nurture along the way.

Ultimately, your greatest resource is yourself. Trust in your knowledge, your network, and your ability to make things happen. You have more potential than you realize, so don't be afraid to leverage your strengths and seek out the resources that will help you achieve your dreams.

CHAPTER 10 - MOTIVATION 101

Motivation is your bonus resource. Motivation is not a fixed trait but a skill that can be cultivated and strengthened. It's the driving force behind our actions, the fuel that propels us towards our goals. Whether you're striving for personal growth, professional success, or simply seeking a more fulfilling life, understanding and harnessing motivation is crucial. At its core, motivation is the willingness to act and the reasons behind those actions. It's not about possessing an innate talent but rather developing a mindset and a set of strategies that enable you to take consistent steps toward your objectives. The key lies in recognizing that action breeds motivation. The more you engage in activities aligned with your goals, the more motivated you'll become to continue and see them through. I believe the way you look at motivation is so important to your goals that I actually (and possibly accidentally) wrote 2 chapters about it.

In this chapter, you will learn how to train yourself to be motivated and what are some enemies of motivation. Motivation is defined as the general desire or willingness of someone to take an action and one's reasons for acting or behaving a particular way. Notice that it isn't defined as a static trait or talent of someone's makeup. This is because motivation is a skill that can be learned like anything else. You read that right. Motivation is a skill. Contrary to popular belief, motivation is not something you just have or not. It is not a gift you have from birth. Motivation is just like any other skill. The more you exercise it, the easier it is to do. You can train yourself to be motivated. In fact, action manifests motivation. The more you complete an action, the more motivated you will become for the action itself, as well as the outcome of said action.

There are several intrinsic forms of motivation that you have inside you already. Some of these key motivators are your own self, the work itself, and the contribution you are making to the world. You are motivated by the self if you are driven by affirmations that focus on your personal identity or belief system of who you are or how you are perceived by others. If the actual work itself is your motivator, you are excited by the adventure of taking the steps toward your goal. If you find yourself thinking, "I want to improve the lives of others." often, odds are you are motivated by the contribution you make in this world.

You can use a habit loop to help create the motivation you need. Compile a list of cues you can use to trigger motivation at any given moment. It can be a playlist, place, exercise, meditation, or anything that gives you the ability to get moving once you activate the habit loop. I use the song "My Shot" from Hamilton. There is something in that song that gets my blood pumping. I must take some action when I listen to it. Thank you, Lin Manuel! I have run many miles thanks to those lyrics playing as loud as I can politely play them on the trails. I have a whole playlist compiled nowadays that gets me fired up. I start every day by listening to it while I get ready. I share the playlist at basketcasebook.com if you're looking for some musical inspiration. Maybe, for you, a quieter moment is more motivating. You can summon your motivation with a quick guided meditation. Again, there is no right way to reach your goals. Go for a run, scream along to some death metal on your lunch break, or do a little warrior posing in the supply closet when you need a pick me up. Just do whatever makes sense for you. You do you, boo.

Once you know how to trick yourself into being motivated even when you don't feel like it, you will be able to take steps toward success every day, regardless of external forces or your feelings.

You will also want to be aware of what demotivates you. Some common demotivators are clutter, avoiding conflicts, and avoidance mechanisms. The space in which you work toward your goals needs to fit the energy you want to create. Clearing the clutter in all areas of your life will free space in your mind as well as your physical environment. Even clear out the email. Busy work and other time-wasting behaviors, like watching hours of TV or scrolling social media, are avoidance mechanisms. Be mindful of when you are doing things just to keep from *having the time* to work on what is actually important. Remember, you make time for what is important in your life. Is watching TikTok for an hour more important than reaching your dreams? Avoiding real or imagined conflict is another way that you might demotivate yourself. When you find yourself trying to keep the peace in any situation, ask yourself what the real reason behind the behavior is. Will keeping the peace truly prevent the conflict and allow you to continue working toward your goals, or are you just putting off the inevitable out of a fear of success, growth, or change? Ask yourself whose peace you are keeping.

Excuses and procrastination have no place on the path to your goals, either. Excuses are the lies we tell ourselves about what is real. They are how we justify procrastination and letting fear hold us back from reaching for success. What do you lie to yourself about? Do you tell yourself that you will start *tomorrow* or that the time just isn't quite right yet? A way to catch yourself in an excuse trap is listening for the word "but". Anytime you hear yourself say "but...." stop right there. Examine yourself. What are you feeling physically? What emotions are you experiencing? What are you afraid of right now? How can you use this information to move forward? What can you do to change your head space?

Replacing every excuse you notice with a commitment will help get you back on track. Commitments are something you are determined to do because you are motivated by a clear and genuine desire for the outcome you have chosen. For example, if you say, "But I don't have time for that", turn it around. Put yourself back in control of the situation by changing it to "I make time for the things that are important to me". I actually love this example because it forces us to be honest about what we truly care about. Being honest and in control of your actions allows you to stay motivated to reach your goals. Another way you can shift your mindset when you don't want to do a particular thing is instead of saying "I have to," change it to "I get to". Instead of "I have to make dinner for the kids," say, "I get to make dinner for the kids." Or "I get to run before work". That one word can make life a little easier some days.

There will be times that you fall into these demotivating behaviors for one reason or another. We all do at some point. You will be able to see these negative outcome habits for what they are more easily when you take the time to assess how your current actions are progressing. Again, this is why regularly scheduled progress assessments are so important. They can have an intense impact on the time frame it takes to reach your goals.

Remember you are in control of your level of motivation. It is not something you just have or don't have. If you find yourself lacking in motivation for any reason, flex your motivation muscles and pump the jam! Clear the demotivators and do whatever actions force the motivation to start oozing out your ears. You can do this. I have faith in you.

I want to add a note here that executive dysfunction is real and not something to beat yourself up over. It is not a lack of motivation. You obviously are motivated while you experience executive dysfunction. You are motivated to do the thing, but you are unable to execute the action. If you are experiencing executive dysfunction often, please reach out to your doctor. THIS IS NOT A PERSONAL FAILURE! Executive dysfunction is not being lazy. It is a medical condition.

CHAPTER 11 – HABITS

Habits are a proclivity to repeat an action or process. Read that again. They are a **choice** to repeat an action or process. Every habit is a choice. Many things that you do in life are a choice, even if you don't realize it. From not being a morning person to the way you put on your big kid underoos. It is easy to forget that the little things are choices, too. You consistently choose to or not to do all the habits in your routine.

According to an article in Psychology Today, there are seven proven steps to forming habits and creating the lasting change you want to see in your life. These steps are reminders, records, rewards, routines, relationships, reflecting, and restructuring. While you are developing a clear plan for the habits you want in your life, keep these 7 things in mind. Leave fun reminders for yourself to encourage you to complete a habit by putting a sticky note in your car or setting an alarm on your phone. Use a habit tracker or journal to keep a record of your accomplishments. Celebrate those accomplishments weekly and/or monthly to reward your own productive behavior. Stick to your routines! Build new strengths into current relationships and create new ones based on the new reliable and trustworthy habits you are creating. Reflect on how your habits are affecting your life and whether you want to restructure a part of your life based on the habits you want to build into your life.

Habits are loops in the stories we tell ourselves about ourselves. They have a trigger that moves you to an action that, in turn, provides a reward for completion. This means that, first, you have a cue or trigger, that is, the reason for a behavior that is then followed by a reward. Trigger. Behavior. Reward. These loops are also referred to as a reward system. The routine this offers can be physical, emotional, or beneficial to the self. The brain processes the reward as worth the effort or not in order to determine if that habit will be used again in the future.

The power of the reward system is the anticipation of or gratitude for the reward. I have found that neurotypicals tend to see the reward as something that comes after effort, whereas many neurodiverse people are more productive upon receiving the reward initially. This is probably due to the need for the ever-elusive dopamine our brains need to feel motivation. Said another way, we either do the work involved to complete the habit loop to receive the reward or celebrate the reward by doing the work. While this may seem obvious, there are many things you do in life that you may not realize that you do purely for the reward, despite the consequences. For instance, you may not realize that you pick fights with your partner for the dopamine hit you get from the makeup sex. Maybe you think the fight is because they literally never put their socks in the hamper, or maybe they always leave the blow dryer in the sink in the morning, but in reality, you want the feeling of closeness that comes from the fun time hormones released during good sex. By looking at the full habit loop, you are better able to see where the flaws are in your story. As Brene Brown says, it's all in the stories that we tell ourselves. Focus on making your stories healthy rather than familiar.

If you start with identifying the trigger, behavior, and reward; you will see in what ways you could shift your mindset about the habit loop to give it a more positive impact in your life. If we use the above example and consider that the reward is the most important, then shifting the behavior could result in a healthier habit loop. Instead of starting the fight, you can initiate a long hug or cuddle session to get your dopamine more positively.

Another example of a habit loop or trigger cycle would be your morning coffee. The cue is waking up, more or less successfully, for the umpteenth day in a row. The behavior is making the coffee. The reward is getting to drink the coffee. Hopefully, alone. And in peace before you must start your day and people begin speaking. This trigger cycle is not inherently good or bad. It is only the process of expressing a habit. You decide if the habit has a positive or negative consequence. Based on the outcome, you judge if the habit is something that should continue in your life or not.

Good or bad? What's the difference? It's all relative, and moderation is usually the key. There is no reason to worry about if a habit is good or bad. We are not in the business of shame or self-sabotage here. You only need to concern yourself with how productive and positive an influence the habit has. Everything you do is for a reason. If you look at your reasoning for each of your habit loops, you may find some areas in your life that you would like to change. Maybe there are a few habit loops that you want to do more often. Maybe a few you could stand to do without.

How do you determine what type of habit you're working with? I'm not a fan of mislabeling anything. This applies to habits as well. Instead of "Is this good or bad?" ask yourself, "Does the habit produce a positive consequence?" such as running a mile every day. Or "Does it produce a negative consequence?" such as smoking a pack of cigarettes daily? If the outcome is positive, then it is likely that it is a "good habit". However, if the outcome is negative, you may want to change or stop the habit altogether. Because one habit may be "good" for one person and "bad" for another, you must only evaluate how the habit presents itself in your life. For instance, a keto diet may cause a positive outcome for one person but has a negative outcome for someone with diabetes. To prevent the feelings of shame that can be associated with some habits, remember to only refer to habits as "positive outcome habits" or "negative outcome habits". I do not want you beating yourself up over the current state of any habit. This book is about your growth. Growth requires reflection and change. Habits are growth in action. There is no room for shame in your growth journey.

Take a few moments each night to recap your day for a week. You are just observing right now. Look to see if it was a productive day. How do you feel about the outcome of your effort each day? Would you do anything differently? List out every habit that you completed each day that had a decided impact on your day. Was it positive, or was it negative? Did you notice anything about your habits or moods that surprised you? After a week or two, you should be able to see your triggers more easily. You may even see some patterns of behavior emerging.

You can now use this data to plan accordingly for the next week. I want you to pick the one positive outcome trigger that you noticed had the most impact on your day. Was it laying out clothes the night before or packing a lunch to take to work? Focus on completing at least one of these positive trigger points every day. Adding a positive trigger will put you one step closer to your desired outcome and create momentum to carry you through the finish line you are working toward.

You will also need to be aware of the triggers that cause negative outcomes. How can you avoid or shift these actions into positive outcomes? For example, if you are doing intermittent fasting and you realize that you wake in the middle of the night for a drink but end up snacking at 2 am because you were in the kitchen, putting a glass of water on the nightstand is a positive trigger adjustment. Or if you have a habit of not crawling out of bed on time that stresses you out during your morning routine, lay out your clothes and make some overnight oats before you go to bed. Small shifts like this create sustainable changes for a lifetime.

Habits can become so ingrained that we forget they are, actually, a choice we make. We have been choosing some habits for so long that we believe that they are a part of our personality, such as dating someone we know is bad for us or hitting the snooze button three too many times every morning. Another example of a habit that you may not realize is really a habit is how you get dressed daily. I bet you put your clothes on in the same way every time. Try changing it up and see how it feels. Just see how different it feels to dress out of order. You still get dressed, but it feels strange. That is how adding new habits can feel in the beginning. Just because you are aware of it doesn't mean it's not working.

 Often, we forget that our habits are a behavior we are choosing to express. In The Effective Life, Stephen Covey tells the story of a ladybug who has forgotten that it can fly. The ladybug franticly crawls back and forth on the palm of a little girl before remembering that it has wings for a reason. Remember your wings. You can choose them any time you remember that they are there to carry you along your way. Just because you are used to crawling around doing something a certain way doesn't mean there aren't more ways to go about doing the task differently. And often with a more desirable result.

A habit that most of us do 100% of the time, even with strangers, is saying "bless you" when someone sneezes. We have done this as a society for so long that most of us forget that saying it is truly a choice we make, not something we must do lest the world end. I recently attended a training summit for Mindvalley. Someone near the stage sneezed a few times. Every time the speaker said, "Bless you." It was such an organic experience to witness a quirky societal habit in that setting. I am not religious, but I hope we never stop random sneeze acknowledgments. Whatever the agreed-upon phrase, can we please, as a society, promise not to quit that habit?

Quitting a habit can be very difficult, especially if you aren't even aware what you are doing is a choice. Take a few minutes to think of some of your daily habits again. Are there any habits you would like to change?

Can you find any that you had forgotten were habits? Pick one of these forgotten or undesirable habits and change it consciously the next time you go to do it. For instance, put your other shoe on first for a week. Or, if you vape but want to quit, add a 2-minute meditation about making healthy choices for your body before you vape. Use the urge to vape, the trigger, to focus on the positive habits that you want to add to your life. Do this every day over the next week or so. Exercise your habit changing muscles on something seemingly trivial. This practice will make shifting the next habits easier to change because your body will be getting used to the unusual feelings of a habit change. You are literally building new neuropathways in your brain. Remember that all habits are only the most frequently used thought highways of the brain to date. It takes 66 days to build a new default highway. A little road construction may be difficult to detour around the first few times, but it will become easier the more times you go there.

Changing a habit, instead of outright quitting, can be a bit easier. This is because, in our brains, the neuropathways we use most often become somewhat fused into our brains. The trigger cycle gets hardwired, and we revert to the neuropathways that are best known when we are triggered. To successfully change a habit, you must change the behavior attached to the cue. For instance, imagine the cue is a looming deadline at work, and the behavior is ordering takeout for lunch, then that leads to a reward of having more time to work on a project. A way to change this behavior into a positive outcome habit is by packing yourself a lunch every day. This allows you to save even more time when you are stressed about the deadline because there is no need to leave work to pick up the takeout. You are also creating more of a reward for yourself by saving money, eating healthier, and potentially having a clearer mind from being about to rest during your break. It will take time to retrain your brain to default to the new behavior. There may be some days that you get the Kung Pao noodles instead of eating the salad you brought from home. You will do this because the default response to the trigger when under stress will, unconsciously, be the earliest founded response. Preparing for the stressors, as best as possible, will help you make the conscious decision to change behaviors when the brain wants the path previously well-traveled. Eventually, the new pathways that you are creating will become the default position.

I know how difficult quitting something outright can be. (CW for next 6 paragraphs: addiction, homelessness, death, body weight, and dysmorphia. The following excerpt is a true story of my life as it relates to how committed you must be to quit a habit. It is not to infer that addiction itself is a habit. Addiction is a disease and should be treated as such.)

I was addicted to meth as a teenager. Meth at any age is a bad idea, but using it at such an important stage of my brain development was especially obtuse. I was using it a lot. A lot. I was self-medicating to cope with unaddressed traumas and body dysmorphia. I did so much meth in the 9ish months that I was heavily using that I got down to 87 pounds. To put that in perspective, I'm 5'9" and weighed about 120 when I started using. I had, thankfully, stopped using initially about 3 months before I became pregnant with my daughter. Weighing in at 87 pounds scared me. I didn't want to die yet, and I knew I must gain some weight. So, I stopped using it. I had changed my behavior with the support of my late husband during that time, but I did not change anything else in my life.

My entire world changed with great expedience in December 2002. Over the course of 12 hours, I went from a pregnant newlywed to a seventeen-year-old widowed mother. My husband died while I was in labor. 2 days after Christmas. 2 weeks before our 1st wedding anniversary. And the day before the life insurance policy was to become active. How do you prepare for that? I still don't know.

As you can imagine, I was under an extreme amount of acute stress that just seemed to spiral even further out of my control. It was during the following 10 months that a *friend* asked several times if I wanted to have just a little meth to get through the struggle of the moment. Of course, I wanted to. I was only able to say no for so long. No longer having the risk of transmission to my child, the urge not to partake was diminished. I slid right back into my old behaviors very easily once my breastmilk had dried up at around 9 months post-partum.

During times of extreme stress, our brains automatically fall back on the easiest (read most used) neuropathway available. A common analogy used to describe these neuropathways is to imagine that they are roads in your brain. The pathways that aren't used often are like the dirt roads of the brain. They are bumpy and narrow, and your thoughts can't travel very fast. The pathways that are regularly used, such as the pathway that is committed to your morning cuppa joe, are likened to interstates. You wake up, and your brain takes over, kicking into autopilot. You could probably make your coffee in your sleep because the neuropathways are so well defined, much like using the cruise control when you hit the open road.

At the time, I didn't understand the science behind habits. I also had no idea what autism was, let alone that I was autistic. Since then, I have spent many, many hours studying how habits affect outcomes in everyday life. I have listened to lectures, taken classes, and read dozens of books on the subject. I'm not an expert, but I'm no dummy when it comes to understanding the way habits work. Over the past 2 ish years, I have begun plowing through all available information on neurodiversity and how it relates to my experience of the world around me. I might not have understood the science of it when I was younger, but I knew this habit of not seeking assistance when necessary and self-medicating to ignore the issues must be stopped before it got out of control again. I knew I would die if I went back down that road, and I could not leave my sweet baby an orphan for any reason. To quit once and for all, I decided that I had to leave everything related to meth behind me. I knew that I wouldn't be able to quit in that environment. That meant I had to move out of state without leaving a forwarding address. I took a tent and the few hundred dollars I had to my name and went for it. I left everyone I knew. Friends and family. Every *safety net* that I had had was gone. I had to find a job, a car, child care, a house all alone and without a phone (or Google). I am grateful to say that it worked. I've been clean and mostly stable for nearly two decades.

Now I do not expect you to take such drastic measures to change your habits, not even if you're addicted. If that is the case though, I urge you to start your journey with getting clean or sober. There are agencies in every state to help you fight the monster that is the disease of addiction. If you need assistance finding a rehab program or other resources and support near you, please dial 211. Remember that YOU ARE WORTHY OF HEALING!

Leaving like I did completely cut me off from the access I had to meth and effectively cut off that behavior possibility immediately. You need not do anything as extreme for most habits that you aim to change. I recommend shifting to new behaviors over time. Baby steps toward new habits are a much more sustainable path to reprograming your brain. When you want to make a sustained change, shifting your behavior is the most productive method. Changing habits is a lifestyle change. A marathon rather than a sprint. Creating positive habits in your life is a long-term commitment.

Sustainability is key when managing your habits. How many times have you or someone you know tried to change something drastically? For instance, the New Year's resolution is notorious for not being a successful form of habit change. This is usually because most people don't understand how to make sustainable changes in their routines with small, regular shifts in behavior rather than a drastic and overwhelming switch.

Studies have shown that *habit stacking* is a gentler and faster way to make significant progress in changing a habit. You may be wondering, "What the heck is habit stacking, Bunni?". Habit stacking is adding a new behavior to your daily schedule by "stacking" it on top of an existing habit. This technique supports the theory that adding a positive outcome habit is more effective than subtracting the negative outcome habits. Imagine a cup of dirty water. If you pour clean water into the cup, even if it doesn't overflow, the dirty water becomes less dense. If you keep pouring clean water into the cup, even as the cup overflows, eventually, all the water in the glass will be clean. This is the same premise, if you keep adding positive outcome habits, eventually you won't have room for negative outcome habits.

An example of a positive outcome habit stack is adding a healthy breakfast while the coffee brews. Instead of staring into the void while you wait for the go-go bean juice to percolate, you can start by adding a slice of toast or a bowl of cold cereal. As it becomes easier to focus on making food you can up your game on what you have for brekkie. You might only start with dry toast and end up with an egg white and veggie omelet with Beyond sausage and buttered toast to eat with coffee every morning.

These types of baby steps will have a lasting and positive impact on your life. You are filling your cup with clear, clean water. Every time you add a positive outcome habit to your daily agenda, you are creating the successful life that you have always dreamt of.

CHAPTER 12 - THE SUPER SIX

Habits are what make up your day-to-day life. In this chapter, we will look at several habits that can make or break your goals, and I'll challenge you to elevate your habit game. Some positive outcome habits that are critical to your daily well-being and longevity are exercise, meditation, hydration, fueling your body, journaling, and keeping a tidy calendar. We'll call them the Super Six Habits for success. A few of these habits may seem trivial to you, but I assure you they are essential for growth.

When you are cultivating a new habit, there are several things to consider. First, it takes about 21 days to make a habit and 66 days for the habit to become the default, automatic behavior. These numbers may be a bit different for those of us who are neurospicy. Don't beat yourself up if it feels like it takes you longer to lock in these habits. Secondly, you want to set yourself up for success. One way to do this is by keeping in mind the quote, "It's easier to hold your principles 100 % of the time than it is to hold them 98% of the time." by Clayton Christensen. 100 % is easier because you don't have to consider the 2% that a 98% person does. Having to decide between the 2% or the 98% can cause decision fatigue (or ego depletion). What is decision fatigue? It is exactly what it sounds like. When you make too many decisions over the course of a day, it uses excess brain energy. The mind becomes tired of making decisions. It's like when your cell phone has Wi-Fi, GPS, Bluetooth, and Sync on at the same time. The battery is depleted faster than if some or all of them were off. As a result, your ability to make decisions is impacted. You won't be able to make decisions as well at the end of your day as when you began. When I first became vegan, I struggled with cheeses. At the time, vegan cheeses weren't as cheese-like as they are today, and I would tell myself that I was "mostly vegan," so it was ok. This struggle was because I had not yet made up my mind to be 100% authentic to myself. Once I decided that I was 100% vegan, it was no longer difficult to choose between with or without cheese. I was vegan. So, I don't eat cheese. Period. It was that easy. All I had to do was commit to my authenticity.

With this in mind, any time you can limit the need to make a decision, you improve your ability to make good decisions. This is because you are conserving brain energy used to make informed decisions. For instance, if you decide that you will start bringing your lunch to work 3 days a week, you will struggle less than if you decide to sometimes bring your lunch. This is because you have given yourself a non-negotiable option. If you don't bring your lunch on Monday or Tuesday, then you know you must bring it the rest of the week. If you make bringing your lunch on Monday, Tuesday, and Thursday every week a nonnegotiable item on your agenda, you save even more decision-making energy. If you bring your lunch on these 3 specific days a week 100% of the time, you don't have to decide between the 98 or 2%. You already know that it is just something you do now. Or don't do it, depending on the objective at the time. Like if you are quitting smoking. I used to smoke. I used to smoke a lot. This was years ago. Well, before I had even gathered my thoughts on habits, let alone been able to articulate them. When I quit, I was smoking 3 ½ packs a day. I know. It's hard to admit that I was smoking so much. But I was. I remember vividly the day I quit. It was December 11th, 2008. I had bronchitis but couldn't afford to go to the doctor for any antibiotics, so I was trying to ride it out. It was frigid and snowing outside. I remember this because I only smoked outside. I distinctly recall thinking how stupid it was for me to be so sick and to go outside into the extreme weather. Especially considering the reason when I could barely breathe as it was. I definitely thought about how dumb it was at the moment. I knew it was gross and didn't want to expose my daughter to secondhand smoke. I stepped out on the porch to have a cigarette before bed. Y'all. I couldn't breathe in deep enough to light the damn cigarette. I tried for a few minutes before giving up. I stomped through the house to the kitchen trash can and slammed my full save 3 cigarettes pack into the bin. My daughter came into the kitchen after hearing me aggressively trudge through the house. She saw that my pack was lying on top of the trash and very cautiously asked what I was doing. Without turning around, and in more clipped a tone than I would like to admit, I said, "I quit smoking!". She asked if I was quitting "forever?". She had seen me try to quit before. I turned around, more in control of my emotions, and defeatedly said, "Yes." She proudly held her pinky high and asked, "Pinky promise?!". How could I refuse? I pinky promised that sweet, cherub-faced 5-year-old and haven't had a cigarette since.

This is why I repeat throughout this book that you must be specific and name things in great, measurable detail to set your intentions and find success every time. By removing the possibility of failure, you instantly become successful. Success becomes inevitable when you name the non-negotiable in detail. Peter Dinklage did exactly this when he decided to walk away from a full-time data processing job to become an actor. He saw the value in himself and realized that half-assing his attempt at acting was not in alignment with his core values and personal mission. He decided in that moment that he was a great actor, and nothing would stop him. Being an actor became his non-negotiable. He was a starving artist for a while getting started, but his efforts would soon pay off. He is best known for his role as the main character, Tyrion Lannister, of what was arguably the greatest television series of all time (obviously pre-last season), Game of Thrones. I'm still waiting for my apology from HBO. Pick your passion and go for it. Call your shot and do it.

Challenge 1

75% of the population of the United States is chronically dehydrated. According to some studies, it's up to a startling 90% in the UK. So, unless you are in that other 10-25%, and kudos to you if you are, drink up. Drinking enough water will nearly instantly give you an edge over your peers. You have likely heard that humans are made of mostly water. Inconveniently, you do have to keep replenishing the water. Once you are drinking enough water, you will notice you can think more clearly and have more energy. Who in this world doesn't want more energy? Next time you reach for a Redbull, grab a water instead. Or at least, grab a water with the energy drink as you are starting out. Habit stacking a glass of water is an easy way to begin hydrating.

Starting today, you will begin drinking a bare minimum of 64 oz of water daily. Half a gallon. It's only 8 glasses of water. This is your first new habit assignment in this book. Remember back to Chapter 11 and the idea of habit stacking. Now is the time to implement this knowledge. When are sometimes you can habit stack a glass of water? Keeping a glass on your bedside table at night can help you get in the minimum daily oz. A glass before your coffee in the morning and before every meal are easy times to add water. Be sure that you finish each glass before drinking anything else, especially beverages that dehydrate the body, like alcohol.

This chapter focuses on adding water and the five other positive outcome habits listed above rather than stopping the negative ones. The reasoning behind this approach is that your mindset, in all things, influences the outcomes in your life. To reach your goals, you must have your shit together. I said what I said. You cannot reach your biggest, wildest dreams if you're riding the Hot Mess Express. You cannot build well on a shoddy foundation. If you want to grow and reach for your dreams, you must set a solid frame to build on. This is not to say that you must have everything figured out in life and be "ready" for your goal. I'm saying you must have a plan for when you open your eyes in the morning most days. Thankfully, the Super Six are pretty simple to implement. They are all things you are at least doing a little bit already. All I am asking is that you do them intentionally from now on.

You will learn to speak to yourself in positive and progressive ways rather than criticism and shame. You will take care of yourself, and you will flourish. You already know you "should" stop doing whatever "bad habit" it is that you're thinking of right now. Anyone telling you to quit isn't going to help. That would only set you up for feelings of shame, negative self-talk and impede your progress. We don't do that here!

Instead, I want you to focus on the healthy and positive changes you want to make in your life. Think about how these changes make you feel and the positivity that comes from implementing them. Think of ways to reward yourself for forming these new habits. Eventually, the positive outcome habits will take up too much of your day for the former negative outcome habits to happen in the first place. According to a 2009 study published in the European Journal of Social Psychology, it takes 66 days for a new behavior to become automatic. A little over 2 months is all it takes until you have rewired your brain into defaulting to the desired habit loop. In the larger scheme of life, 2 months is but a blink in your life. You can totally do that. I have faith in you.

Challenge 2

Have you ever been told not to think about something? It doesn't work. You literally cannot NOT think of the one thing you aren't supposed to think of. It's commonly referred to as the "white bear theory" in your entry-level psychology classes. Here's an example of the theory. Don't think of an orange flamingo playing hopscotch. I bet you've never had that thought before I told you not to. Instead of attempting not to think of the flamingo in all its hopscotch glory, accept that the thought will come. We cannot prevent thoughts from coming into our minds.

However, we can control what we do with our thoughts once they arrive.

If you train yourself to see the flamingo as your cue to start seeing a purple pony leaping over the flamingo and running in a new direction, you, too, will be able to move in a new direction. I understand that this example is ludicrous, but by using the new habit, you take control back in your mind and life. Watch the flamingo thoughts being replaced by the new thought waves. If I told you to focus on stopping your negative habits, all you would have is negative outcome or "bad" habits. However, by putting all your effort into the new, positive outcome habits, you automatically think of the old habits less. Let your purple ponies lead you to the new habits you want to have. It's another win-win situation for you.

Congrats. You just started your second habit challenge. If you allow a thought to come into your mind, acknowledge it, and let it go or correct the thought pattern to the desired thoughts, you are meditating. Really. That's it. Your challenge is to do this for at least 10 minutes a day. You can do this in the morning, at night, on a break at work, in the tub, or on a walk in the park. Anywhere and anytime. Except probably not while operating heavy machinery. I do not recommend meditation while driving any type of vehicle. But you can drink water. See what I did there?

Challenge 3

Your next habit challenge is to tidy your calendar to set your routine up for success. Delete the junk. Add the important stuff. Remember that if it isn't in the calendar, it doesn't exist. Set reminders to drink your water, take your meds, go to bed on time, exercise, and to review your personal statements from Chapter 3. Add all the early dismissals for your children's school days for the whole year. Any reoccurring doctors' appointments. The soccer game dates. Your bowling league tourneys. Add the dates you want to check your progress toward your goals. Put in the celebration dinner at your favorite restaurant for when you reach your next goal post. Setting everything into your calendar creates organization out of the chaos of chasing goals, and it will give you the routine to reach those goals at exponential rates. Become a chaos coordinator. Having everything in the calendar leaves space in your brain to focus on what is at hand. Writing it all down is also a trigger to get your RAS, reticular activating system, on board as well. More on that later.

Challenge 4

Journaling is the next habit challenge on your agenda. You can journal however you see fit. You can use a captain's log style journal or go full-on "Dear Diary...". Whatever gets you to write something about your day every day.

I do a combo journal. I write down 10 affirmations and 5 little things that I am grateful for in the morning as I reflect on the previous day and what I must do for today. Starting the day with a sense of gratitude and passion makes all the difference in my level of production. I have a reminder to look for the positives in my day because I know that tomorrow I will be writing down the good of today. You will find what you seek. If you seek the good in each day, you will find a multitude of things to be grateful for. Jotting down the 10 affirmations that I am currently working on every morning helps to keep them on top of my mind as I navigate through my days.

In the evening, before bed, I keep a journal that is more of a captain's log to keep track of my growth and progress. I want to have a tangible record of my struggles and successes. This way I can look back to see how far I have come whenever I become disenchanted with the road I am currently traveling. We know that motivation is a result of action. When I need to get motivated, I can turn through the pages and see a chronological timeline of how far I have come already. This usually lights the fire in my belly again, and I can move forward.

Your next two challenges are just as important to your health and physical well-being as getting enough water. To perform at your personal best, you must take care of your body. Fueling your body and your exercise regimen are critical to your overall well-being. I'm not saying you need to go vegan too or start running 10 miles daily just for funsies. What I am saying is that you need to get enough nutrition and sleep for your body to function and think properly, as well as enough movement for your body to remember it is actually a body that can do incredible things.

Challenge 5

Challenge 5 is to fuel your body for optimal functionality. Nutrition and sleep are your body's fuel—the gas to your proverbial tank. Too much or too little of either can have catastrophic effects on your body, mood, and mind.

The average person needs 7-9 hours of sleep. If you are not getting at least this much sleep at once, go to bed earlier. You deserve to be well-rested. There is no other way to attack the day all bright-eyed and bushy-tailed. There are many excuses you may tell yourself as to why you don't need that much sleep. Stop lying to yourself. You do need the rest. Your body uses sleep as a time to process the events of the day and to restore your vitality. Your body fights off diseases and helps to heal you while you sleep. Meditation before bed is a great way to calm the mind down for bed. The last thing you want is to be lying in bed, thinking about how you aren't sleeping. Like everything else, there are many apps to help you sleep well. There are even some that can track your sleep. If you are having trouble sleeping and have tried using fewer stimulants, sleep aids, and going to bed earlier to no avail, consult your doctor. Insomnia is a real mood and energy killer.

If you have access to a nutritionist, use that privilege. If not, look for an app that meets your nutritional needs. There is an app for every kind of dietary need you have. Diabetic? Need to lose weight? Need to gain weight? Want to try keto? Are you into intermittent fasting? Calorie counting? Just want to track your macros? THERE'S. AN. APP. FOR. THAT. Make sure you are getting the nutrition your brain and body need in any way that you can. You will feel so much better and have the energy to tackle any goal on your list if you feed your inner beast mode.

Challenge 6

Your exercise challenge is to move for 30 minutes more than you usually do every single day. Yes, every day. Even on Monday and Wednesday and hungover on Saturday, too. Unless you have the actual plague, you need to move your body. Get up and go for a walk before work. Or go for a quick jog in the evening. Take the stairs. Dance around the house while blasting 90s rap as you clean up from the day. Whatever gets you moving your body more than you were before reading this book. Move as you are able. (If your body isn't able to move traditionally, do mind exercises like math puzzles or trivia games. Just do what YOU can.) Work up to 30 minutes at a time if you need to. Just make sure you are doing more than you were before. If my blind mom can get in her 30 minutes of movement daily, then I bet you can find a way too! Set your timer for 30 minutes and shake, shake, shake, Senora! Shake your body line!

.

In this chapter, you have been challenged a lot. You may have never before considered intentionally doing any number of the super six tasks you've faced in these pages. To become more successful in your life you must take control of your life. Mastering these 6 tasks is the key to conquering all that life puts in your way. Starting today with water, add every new challenge to your calendar. Remember that if it's not in the calendar, it doesn't exist. Set the start date for 21 days apart for each of the Super Six habits. For example, if you start drinking water on Feb 13th, then your next habit will start on Mar 6th. Once you have added all 6 habits to your calendar, add a celebration date for 66 days of doing your new habits. In keeping with the water starting date used in this example, your celebration date is April 20th. Rewards are a real driver of habit motivation. Use this knowledge as a great "excuse" to celebrate all your successes.

As you work your way through this book and the strife of working toward your goals, you will see the importance of laying the foundation created by the Super Six. The Super Six, combined with your personal code of ethics, core values, and mission statement, will give you everything you need to reach for any goal you can imagine.

CHAPTER 13 — CARING FOR YOU

As I emphasized in the previous chapter, your routine is the foundation of your success. It's where the daily battles are won and lost. However, as crucial as your routine is, it's equally important to recognize the value of rest and recovery. In fact, there are moments when downtime is not just important but essential—perhaps even more vital than the active time you spend working toward your goals.

Rest and recovery are the times when you pause to catch your breath, reflect on your journey, and allow yourself the space to heal and rejuvenate. Downtime is your opportunity for introspection and self-care. After reaching a significant milestone—whether it's the summit of a major goal or a smaller goalpost along the way—it's important to take a break. This break allows you to regroup, assess where you stand on your path, and decide what the next step should be. Use this time not only to relax but also to celebrate your accomplishments. Every victory, no matter how small, deserves recognition.

Celebrating your successes reinforces your daily habits. By giving yourself a moment to acknowledge the hard work you've put in, you create a positive feedback loop. Each time you celebrate, you're rewarding yourself for the effort and dedication it took to get there. This acknowledgment is crucial because it helps silence the inner critic, that voice of self-doubt that feeds imposter syndrome. You deserve to pat yourself on the back, to take pride in what you've achieved, and to recognize that every step forward is a victory.

That said, it's important to distinguish between after-care and self-care. While after-care is a form of self-care, focusing solely on after-care can lead to burnout, especially if you're not regularly incorporating routine self-care into your life. True self-care involves taking an active role in improving your health, well-being, and happiness, particularly during times of stress or struggle. It's about doing things that nourish you, both physically and mentally, and that replenish your energy so you can continue moving forward.

Self-care can take many forms, and it's important to find what works best for you. Whether it's keeping a journal, indulging in a hot bubble bath after a long day, scheduling a massage, or simply getting a good night's sleep, these acts of self-care are essential to your overall well-being. Even something as simple as treating yourself to a small reward, like a little retail therapy or spending time with friends, can be a meaningful way to care for yourself. The key is to make self-care a regular part of your routine, something you do daily, not just when you're feeling overwhelmed or burnt out.

Having a consistent self-care routine does more than just nourish your body and mind; it also sets a powerful precedent for how others should treat you. When you make self-care a priority, you send a clear message that you value yourself and your well-being. This kind of commitment to self-respect naturally establishes boundaries, as it signals to others that you won't tolerate treatment that falls below the standards you've set for yourself. When you regularly engage in self-care, you cultivate a sense of self-worth that is reflected in your interactions with others. People learn to respect your time, energy, and emotional space because they see that you respect these aspects of yourself. By consistently practicing self-care, you not only recharge and protect your energy but also reinforce the expectation that others should honor and respect your boundaries. This creates a ripple effect, where the care you give to yourself elevates the care and respect you receive from the world around you.

You've probably heard it said that we're not made for constant growth, that it's impossible to be in a perpetual state of expansion. While I understand where this sentiment comes from, I see things a bit differently. Growth doesn't always look like forward motion. There are times when it may seem like we're standing still, but in reality, we're gathering strength and knowledge, refilling our internal reserves. Just like wildflowers have their seasons—some for blooming and others for gathering energy—so do we. Both phases are essential for our well-being and progress. Even the tallest tree needs deep roots to stand tall, so don't mistake your periods of rest and reflection for stagnation. These are the times when you're nurturing your roots, preparing for the next phase of growth.

Resting is not a sign of weakness or failure; it's an essential part of the journey. Take that bubble bath, read that book, blast your favorite guilty pleasure playlist, and allow yourself the time you need to refill your glass before you take on your next challenge. Remember, you can't pour from an empty cup. Recharging your energy is as important as any other part of your routine. Without it, you'll find yourself running on fumes, unable to give your best to anything or anyone.

We all need rest, and it's important to recognize that rest comes in many forms. There are several types of rest that we need to incorporate into our lives: physical rest, mental rest, creative rest, sensory rest, social rest, and spiritual rest. Each type of rest serves a different purpose and fulfills a different need.

Physical rest is the most obvious—it's about giving your body a break. This could mean getting a full night's sleep, taking a refreshing nap, or enjoying a leisurely walk during your lunch break. Mental rest, on the other hand, is about giving your mind a break. This could involve reading a good book, watching a comforting movie, or meditating. Creative rest is about stepping away from the demands of constant innovation and allowing your mind to wander—sometimes, this can be as simple as spending time outdoors or engaging in a relaxing hobby. Sensory rest involves reducing the stimuli around you—turning off the bright lights, lowering the volume, and just letting your senses relax. Social rest is about spending time with those you care about, doing things that bring joy without the pressures of daily life. Finally, spiritual rest connects you to something larger than yourself, whether through religious practices, community involvement, or personal reflection.

Being aware of these different types of rest helps you take a more holistic approach to your well-being. Life isn't just about checking off boxes on a to-do list; it's about experiencing life in all its dimensions. We are complex, multifaceted beings with a wide range of needs, and recognizing these needs allows us to lead fuller, more joyful lives.

Another important aspect of self-care is reflection. Take the time to check in with yourself regularly. Ask yourself important questions: Are you healthy? Are you happy? Do you feel supported and loved by those around you? Are you able to support and love them in return? Are you safe? Are you able to make time for yourself and the things that matter most to you? These questions help you stay grounded and ensure that you're taking care of yourself in a meaningful way.

As you move forward and implement these practices in your life, take a moment to reflect on your journey. After you've achieved a goal and taken the time to rest and refuel, ask yourself a few key questions: Did you notice any changes or growth? Did your journey unfold as you expected, or were there surprises along the way? Were there challenges that turned out to be easier or harder than you anticipated? What did you learn that might help you as you pursue future goals? Did you realize that activities like journaling, meditating, and keeping your schedule organized are also forms of self-care? Reflecting on these questions after each goal allows you to grow and become better equipped for the challenges that lie ahead.

Finally, remember that self-care is not a luxury—it's a necessity. It's your responsibility to care for yourself first and foremost. If you've ever flown on a commercial flight, you've heard the safety announcement: "Put on your oxygen mask first before assisting others." This is because you can't help anyone else if you're like, ya know, not breathing yourself. Self-care is just as important as oxygen, even if the consequences of neglecting it aren't as immediately apparent. The world needs you to be the best version of yourself, and that means making self-care a priority. By doing so, you're not only taking care of yourself but also ensuring that you can continue to contribute to the lives of those around you. We're all counting on you to be at your best, and that starts with taking care of yourself. Embrace your best self. Glow up daily.

CHAPTER 14 — ON THE DAILY

A daily constitution that works for you is crucial for reaching your goals. In this chapter, we will take a look at where your habits and behaviors currently are and what you can do to shift them into a routine that is impossible not to do. Well-planned routines remove failure as an option. A well-kept calendar allows for an easy, regular routine. You can see when and where each habitual part of your routine should take place. Conquering your day-to-day life makes the life of your dreams inevitable.

A routine is a collection of easily repeated habits. Having a regular routine is a peremptory factor when choosing to accomplish your goals. A routine allows you the freedom to reach your goals by making time to work on them. Taking a step every day, however minute, toward your goals will inevitably see you to your destination. It is a simple yet powerful natural consequence of forward momentum. Physics holds, as a fact, that an object in motion will stay in motion. The same is true for you.

Some days, you will be sailing through everything as though the day were made for you. However, some days, just putting your feet on the floor is a struggle. I'm here to tell you the struggle is real. Like, really real. Frfr. This is because most motivation occurs after the action. More often than not, you must first do the thing before you want to do the thing. But once you have the ball rolling, you want to keep moving. Momentum is motivating. Refer to chapters 10 and 21 on motivation. (Yes. There are two chapters on motivation. It is that important.)

As some of you doubtlessly know, I endure a full house of chronic conditions. I, as patiently as possible, endure the pains. I wait through the waves of pain and darkness that too often seem to be at every step. I am so grateful that I have found the patience that comes from years of battle in a war that never ends. It was in the throes of that battle in which this book was born.

I have fibromyalgia and chronic fatigue. If you share the unfortunate luck of having fibromyalgia as well, you understand what a cruel sense of humor the body can have. If not, imagine you had the flu and got hit by a bus, you will never feel 100% again, and just for fun, most people AND

MANY DOCTORS don't believe what you are going through. *Insert eyeroll here*

During a particularly rough fibromyalgia flare, I was barely able to walk, and the fibro fog (a symptom that causes a sort of detached mental feeling with limited access to short- or long-term memory) was causing me to forget what I was saying midsentence. I was a truck driver at the time, and thankfully, I had a few days off to rest. My beagle, Zoey, was attempting to take me for a walk when the light bulb turned on. I never made the kind of progress that I wanted when I was working toward multiple things. On the contrary, when I had one thing that had to be done, I was able to make great strides toward success in a very timely manner.

 In fact, I went from working at Starbucks full-time to a full-grown semi-truck driver in five weeks because of the focus and drive I was able to put into the change. I understood the level of commitment that was going to be necessary to complete such a feat and quit my job at Starbucks to study full-time for the driver's test. To give you a point of reference, it takes an average of 3 months for most people to obtain a commercial driver's license. I have since learned that I have ADHD and autism, so hyper-focus is a superpower that I possess. Unfortunately, I also suffer from ED, so it evens out. Not THAT ED. Executive dysfunction is the fun thing where you want to do the thing, but your brain refuses to allow you to do the thing. ED is truly infuriating.

During that walk, I realized the problem is having a "plan B". Plan B requires planning for Plan A to fail. Having a plan B is literally planning to fail. I'll say that again for those of you in the back, HAVING A PLAN B IS LITERALLY PLANNING TO FAIL.

Who does that?! Well, most people do. But not you. Not anymore.

You want to set yourself up for success. You do this by setting up a solid routine. To do so, you may need to rewire this part of your brain. I promise it's not as difficult as it sounds. The brain is a wild, dense mass of neuropathways that control how we live and see the world. The more frequently a neuropathway is used, the more it will be used without a conscious decision to do so. When you notice a way of thinking that you want to change, you will have to shift to a new neuropathway. You can create a routine that meets your needs even if you are also neurospicy. You just might need to get a bit creative while setting it up initially.

One of the ways I trick myself into creating new neuropathways was inspired by my ex-partner. He is big on analogies. One day, when I was having a difficult time, he told me to think of my brain as a juice bar. I have the ability to make an infinite combination of outcomes based on the ingredients or the thoughts and actions I choose. I can choose which ingredient combination to adjust the flavors. I can choose which outcomes I want by adjusting what actions and efforts I put into moving through my days. If I use the same ingredients that I have been using over and over again, I will get the same outcomes. If I come at a problem or discussion the same way that I always have, nothing will change. The "juice" stays the same. However, if I adjust the combination of ingredients, I may produce a new juice, or outcome, that suits the situation in a measurably more positive way.

The neurotransmitters and receivers in our brains remember the path they have been taking and try to use the path of least resistance as often as possible. Some days, it is easier than others to pause and take a step back from myself and the emotions that I am wrapped up in. However, if I can just take a moment to breathe and look at the "juice bar" of my mind, I can often make a small shift that makes all the difference in my results.

By remembering to look at the juice bar, you will make more progress in creating new habits and letting go of the negative outcome habits that you no longer wish to keep in your life. What shifts in your behaviors and thoughts could be beneficial to the juice recipes of your mind?

When I left Starbucks, I was trying out a new juice recipe. I created a new routine in which I spent the time I would have been slinging espresso shots practicing driving and backing a semi. Because my routine changed so drastically, I was able to achieve a large goal in my life. I went all in on the risk and was able to reach the goal much faster than if I had just dipped my toe in the water. Changing my routine was the key to growing the momentum that created the motivation to get through the hard days.

What areas of your routine do you already have set? Do you have a routine that you follow proactively, or do you sort of just react to your day as it comes? You will find that you have more time to do what it is that you want to be doing if you set your routine to be proactive. You will want to focus on your morning and evening routines to begin with.

Once you have those figured out, you can work on reworking your full daytime routine to accommodate more time to focus on your goals.

Your morning routine is how you set the tone for the whole day. You want to set it up so that you are in control of your day. You may want to start getting up 30 minutes to an hour earlier than you have been. Use this time to get in front of your day. Look at your calendar to see what obligations you have for the day. Take time for your morning journal entry. Reflect on how yesterday went. What worked well, and what could have been better? How will you make today a better experience? Remember, you are your only competition. You are striving to be a better you than you were yesterday. If you need to go to bed earlier to be a better you, your routine is how you make that possible. Your routine is how you will reach your goals.

CHAPTER 15 - FAILURES

Failure is a heavy word. It is wrapped in negative emotions, from disappointment to shame. Don't let the fear of failure hold you back. Every screw-up, every whoops, and every "Damn it!" is just another stepping stone on your path to success. As Brain Tracy wisely said, "It is not failure that holds you back; it is the fear of failure that paralyzes you." I've said it before but it is as true today as the first time I said it. It is ok to be afraid. It is not okay to let that stop you from doing the thing. Take a deep breath and do the thing.

You might be wondering about "what if" you fail at something. What if you stumble? You may think that succeeding 100% of the time is impossible. And depending on your outlook, you could be right. The goal of this book is to keep moving forward until you reach success. You've just got to focus. FOCUS- Follow One Course Until Successful. There will undoubtedly be times along the way that don't go as planned. Some people will see these as a failure and just throw in the towel. They will go ahead and quit. They will give up. But we don't do that there here. This method is not for the faint of heart.

Channel your "inner baby". (I'm shaking my head at myself for typing that out right along with you, but try to follow along, please.) Think about when a baby is learning to walk. They don't just stand up and walk perfectly right out the gate. They lean on the coffee table. They hold onto the couch. Their adorable little legs wobble like Aunt Wanda's Jello mold at the family reunion. They fail fifty-eleven times before they ever get the first step on their resume. Then they fall a bazillion times during the toddler years before they have walking more or less mastered. Then the cute little idiots decide to try something else previously never achieved. Babies and toddlers are the reigning champions of failure, and it doesn't stop them from doing it. Given they usually have a better support system and haven't been taught how to be embarrassed yet. So, pretend you are a giant baby and freaking try to do it. So what if you don't get it perfectly on the first try? Try again. And again, until you figure it out.

A setback is only a failure if you give up. The trick to never failing is to never, ever give up. You want to fail forward. You can see these missteps as the stepping stones that they are. Each stepping stone gets you that much closer to success. You may recall that Edison once said, "I didn't fail 1000 times. The light bulb was an invention with 1000 steps.". Imagine if Edison or any of the thinkers of the time had given up on the idea itself after finding so many ways that it didn't work. How many inventions that make your life easier on a daily basis may never have come to pass if the inventors had given up when it didn't work the very first 27 times? We probably wouldn't have electric toothbrushes or razors, televisions, cellphones, or even zippers. Can you imagine life without zippers? It is wild to think about how the smallest inventions may never have happened and how different our lives would be without them.

One method of dealing with failure is to prevent it in the first place. An ounce of prevention is worth a pound of cure. One way to prevent failure is to be specific and to name everything you do. This is important. By being as specific as possible in everything you do, you can prevent many failures.

Sometimes, change can feel like a failure, too. That is only the fear talking. Change can be difficult and sometimes scary. Change is constant, complex, and often rapid. Many times in your life, a change will be made that is outside your control. In these instances, you must remember to be proactive, not reactive. You may be afraid but do not react. You will want to react immediately, sometimes. Take a breath and wait to respond. Only respond, never react. Sleep on it, as they say. An advantage you have just from being human is the ability to be prospective. Prospection is the ability to generate and evaluate any number of possible futures. You can evaluate a situation and several of the possible outcomes from choosing any given path. By pausing for prospection instead of reacting, you are automatically ahead in the game. This pause gives you the perspective to make the choice that best suits the goal you are working toward. Practicing meditation will make it easier to be proactive in your thoughts and habits.

When you look at a failure in this way, you are more likely to find a way to move forward using the "failure" as a step along your path instead of letting it become an ending of the path itself.

Many thousands of goals have been reached only after numerous "failures". Don't let a small failure be your end game. When life trips you up, roll with it. Dust yourself off and stand back up. If you fall down seven times, get up eight. Keep taking the steps to reach your goals. Every time something doesn't go quite as planned, examine it. See what went wrong. Adjust the course to compensate for the newfound knowledge and make another move. In doing so, the failure becomes a learning experience and just another step on your path to eventual success. It is in this way that failure ceases to exist. Without failure, success becomes inevitable.

CHAPTER 16 – EN ROUTE

Let's embark on a comprehensive exploration of the distinctions between your purpose, plan, and goal. These concepts are vital to understanding and navigating the path to success in any facet of life. By delving deeply into each of these elements, you can harness their power to create a life of intentionality, progress, and fulfillment.

Understanding Your Purpose: What makes you tick

Your purpose is the cornerstone of everything you do; it is the reason behind your actions, the driving force that compels you to pursue certain activities and goals. Your purpose is what fuels the fire in your belly. However, it's more than just a reason—it's a profoundly ingrained emotion, a burning passion that drives your behavior and decisions. Purpose gives you the enthusiasm to wake up every morning with a sense of direction and determination. It's where your inner fire is ignited, creating the drive that sustains you even during challenging times when motivation alone might not suffice.

When you operate from a place of purpose, you are no longer merely going through the motions of life. Every action is an act of creation. You are not just working toward a goal because it's something you think you should do; you are working toward it because it aligns with your core values, desires, and personal mission. This alignment transforms mundane tasks into significant milestones, each contributing to the larger picture of your life's journey.

Moreover, purpose acts as a guiding star in times of uncertainty or difficulty. When obstacles arise, as they inevitably will, your purpose serves as a beacon that keeps you moving toward your dreams. It provides clarity and direction, helping you to navigate challenges with resilience and grace. Without a clear sense of purpose, it's easy to become lost or discouraged, especially when faced with setbacks. But with purpose, even the most difficult tasks become manageable as you understand their role in fulfilling your greater mission in life.

Purpose is also the source of your passion, the fuel that powers your journey. It is the underlying reason that you feel compelled to pursue certain goals or take specific actions. This passion is contagious; it not only motivates you but can also inspire those around you. When others see how deeply committed you are to your purpose, they are more likely to support and encourage you in your endeavors. This support network further amplifies your ability to achieve your most outrageous goals.

The Path: Charting Your Course with Intention

Once you clearly understand your purpose, the next step is to chart a course that will lead you to your goals. Traditionally, this course is referred to as a "plan." However, in this discussion, I prefer to use the term "path" instead of "plan," as it better encapsulates the fluid, dynamic nature of the journey you are about to undertake.

The term "plan" often brings rigid structures and fixed outcomes to mind. We are all too familiar with the saying, "Plans fail," and this notion can instill a sense of fear and hesitation. If a plan fails, what happens next? Does that mean you have failed as well? The answer is a resounding no. You do not fail; you adapt, adjust, and continue moving forward. This is why I advocate for the concept of a path—an evolving, adaptable route that leads you toward your goals rather than a fixed plan that may crumble at the first sign of adversity.

Think of your path as a journey through a countryside you have yet to explore. The terrain may change, the weather may shift, and unforeseen obstacles may arise, but as long as you remain committed to your destination, you will find a way to keep moving forward. This mindset allows for flexibility and resilience. Instead of being rigidly attached to a specific plan, you can adjust your course as needed, making detours or even taking a completely new route if the situation demands it. The path is not about perfection; it's about progress. One more step forward.

Your path is something you create with intention and purpose. It is not a one-size-fits-all blueprint; instead, it is a personalized route that you design based on your unique goals, strengths, experiences, and circumstances. This path is your guide, your roadmap to success, but it is not set in stone. You have the power to modify it, add or remove steps as necessary, and ensure that it remains aligned with your purpose and goals.

By thinking of your journey as a path rather than a plan, you liberate yourself from the pressure of sticking to a predefined set of actions. Instead, you can focus on the overarching goal you are striving to achieve. This shift in perspective transforms the way you approach your journey. You are no longer just following a plan; you are navigating a path, one that you have the power to shape and direct. You naturally have more agency in the outcome when you pay attention to the power of the language you use to define your world.

Defining Your Goals: The Mountains in Your Journey

Now that you have identified your purpose and charted your path, it's time to focus on your goals—the specific milestones you aim to achieve along the way. Your goals are the tangible outcomes you are working toward, the summits that you strive to reach. However, goals are not merely endpoints; they are dynamic, evolving targets that guide your progress and keep you moving forward.

To better understand the nature of your dreams, imagine a vast mountain range, each peak representing a different goal in your life. Just as every mountain is unique in shape, size, and terrain, so too is each goal. Some goals may be small and easily attainable, like rolling hills that you can cross with minimal effort. Others may be towering and formidable, like jagged peaks that require significant preparation, effort, and perseverance to conquer.

In this analogy, each goal is a mountain to be climbed, a summit to be reached. This visualization is powerful because it allows you to focus on one goal at a time, just as you would focus on reaching the summit of one mountain before moving on to the next. This approach encourages a mindset of focused, deliberate action. You don't have to abandon your other goals to pursue the one in front of you; instead, you can prioritize and tackle them sequentially, ensuring that each one receives the attention it deserves.

This process of climbing one mountain at a time fosters a sense of progress and achievement. Each goal you reach is a stepping stone to the next, building momentum and confidence as you continue your journey. This sequential approach also helps to prevent overwhelm, as you can concentrate your energy and resources on the goal at hand, knowing that the others will be addressed in due course.

However, it's essential to recognize that reaching a goal is rarely easy, even if the path to it is clear. The journey to the summit requires dedication, effort, and a willingness to keep going, even when the climb becomes steep and challenging. This is where the concept of the path becomes crucial. By focusing on your path—your carefully designed route to the summit—you can navigate the obstacles that arise, making steady progress toward your goal.

Rescripting Your Journey: From "Plan A" to "Goal 1"

One of the most transformative shifts you can make in your goal-setting approach is to rescript the way you think about your journey. This involves moving away from the traditional notion of "Plan A" and instead embracing the idea of "Goal 1." This subtle change in language may seem insignificant at first, but it carries profound implications for your mindset and approach to success.

When you think in terms of "Plan A," there is an inherent assumption that there is also a "Plan B," "Plan C," and so on—backup plans in case the first one fails. This mindset can create a sense of divided focus as you constantly consider the possibility of failure and the need for alternative plans. It can also lead to a scattergun approach, where you spread your energy and attention across multiple plans, none of which receive the full commitment they deserve.

In contrast, when you think in terms of "Goal 1," you are committing yourself fully to the task at hand. There is no backup plan because you don't need one. You have a clear path, and you are focused on reaching the summit of this goal before moving on to the next. This singular focus is compelling, as it allows you to channel all your energy, attention, and resources into achieving one goal at a time.

The mere existence of "Goal 1" implies that there will be a "Goal 2" and "Goal 3," but each one will be tackled in its own time, in its own sequence. This approach fosters a sense of order and progression, allowing you to move through your goals with purpose and clarity. You are not jumping from one plan to another, hoping that something will stick; instead, you are methodically climbing one mountain at a time, confident that each step you take brings you closer to your ultimate vision.

This shift in mindset also empowers you to reject the notion of failure. In the traditional "Plan A" mindset, failure is always a looming possibility, something to be avoided at all costs. However, in the "Goal 1" mindset, there is no failure—only progress. If you encounter obstacles or setbacks, you adjust your path and keep moving forward. Each challenge becomes an opportunity to learn and grow rather than a potential pitfall that could derail your entire journey.

The Power of Routine: Building a Foundation for Success

While purpose, path, and goals are the guiding elements of your journey, your daily routine serves as the foundation that supports them. A well-crafted routine is critical to your success, ensuring that you consistently take the necessary actions to move closer to your goals. However, a routine does not mean micromanaging every minute of your day; instead, it involves establishing essential habits and practices that become non-negotiable parts of your daily life.

These routine tasks, though seemingly small, have a significant impact on your overall progress. Just as brushing your teeth is essential for maintaining good oral hygiene, specific daily actions are crucial for maintaining momentum and productivity on your path to success. These tasks should be short, manageable, and directly aligned with your goals. They are the building blocks of your journey, and their cumulative effect can be profound.

One powerful concept to incorporate into your routine is the one-minute rule, popularized by Gretchen Rubin. This rule suggests that if a task takes less than one minute to complete, you should do it immediately. This simple strategy can have a transformative effect on your productivity and mental clarity. Addressing small tasks as they arise prevents them from piling up and becoming overwhelming. This frees up mental space and creates a sense of accomplishment and momentum that carries over into other areas of your life.

For example, imagine the mental relief of not worrying about small, nagging tasks like responding to a quick email, putting a dish in the dishwasher, or hanging up your coat. By dealing with these tasks immediately, you reduce stress and create more time and energy to focus on your larger goals. Additionally, by maintaining a clutter-free environment—both physically and mentally—you may find that you sleep better at night, which in turn enhances your productivity the next day.

Routine tasks, when consistently practiced, lead to what I call "compounding productivity." Just as compound interest in a retirement account grows exponentially over time, these small, daily actions accumulate and multiply, leading to significant progress in the long run. For instance, a simple habit like making your bed every morning can set a positive tone for the day, giving you a sense of accomplishment and motivation to tackle more significant tasks. Over time, these small victories add up, creating a powerful momentum that propels you forward on your path to success.

(A quick note for my fellow neurodivergent thinkers: Before you dive into a one-minute task, make sure you remember what you were doing before you started. It's all too easy to get sidetracked by micro-tasks and lose track of your main objective. You might consider keeping a special list of these micro-tasks to tackle all at once later, or simply jot down what you were doing so you can return to it without missing a beat.)

A Rising Tide Lifts All Boats: The Ripple Effect of Progress

As you make progress toward your goals, you will begin to notice a ripple effect in other areas of your life. This phenomenon is beautifully captured in the phrase, "A rising tide lifts all boats." Just as the tide raises the water level in a harbor, lifting all the boats within it, progress in one area of your life can lead to improvements in other areas as well.

For example, as you become more disciplined in your routine and consistently achieve your goals, you may find that your overall sense of well-being improves. You may experience increased energy, better focus, and a greater sense of purpose in your daily life. This positive momentum can spill over into your relationships, your career, and your personal growth, creating a virtuous cycle of success and fulfillment.

Trusting this process is key to maintaining momentum and staying committed to your path. When you understand that each small step you take is contributing to a larger, cumulative effect, you are more likely to stay motivated and focused, even when the progress seems slow. It's important to remember that success is not always about grand gestures or dramatic changes; often, it's the small, consistent actions that make the most significant impact over time.

In conclusion, the journey of purpose, path, and goals is a powerful framework for achieving success in any area of your life. By understanding and embracing each of these elements, you can create a life of intentionality, progress, and fulfillment. Your purpose is the driving force behind your actions, providing the motivation and direction you need to keep moving forward. Your path is the dynamic, adaptable route that guides you toward your goals, allowing you to navigate challenges with resilience and grace. Your goals are the tangible milestones that mark your progress, the summits you strive to reach as you continue on your journey.

By rescripting your approach from "Plan A" to "Goal 1," you empower yourself to focus on one goal at a time, confident that each step you take is bringing you closer to your ultimate vision. This mindset shift fosters a sense of progress and achievement, allowing you to navigate your journey with purpose and clarity. By establishing a solid daily routine, you create a foundation of consistent, productive habits that support your path and propel you toward success.

As you continue on this journey, remember that each small step you take, each goal you achieve, contributes to a larger, cumulative effect that can transform your life. Trust the process, stay committed to your purpose, and embrace the power of focus and intentionality. There is no limit to what you can achieve when you set yourself up for success.

CHAPTER 17 - THE MOUNTAIN RANGE

Choosing your goal can be both an exhilarating and daunting experience. The excitement comes from the possibility of achieving something significant, while the fear often stems from the uncertainty of the journey ahead. I find it helpful to envision each goal as a mountain summit, a peak that stands tall, representing your ultimate achievement. Just as each mountain is unique, with its own set of challenges and paths, so too are your goals. No two are alike, and the path you take to reach each summit will vary. It's essential to remember that you can only climb one mountain at a time, just as you should focus on one goal at a time.

In this analogy, your one big goal is the summit. The smaller, more manageable steps that guide you toward the summit are your goalposts. The tasks that bridge the gap between these goalposts are your mile markers, and the overall journey you embark on to reach the summit is your map. This map is your guide, your plan of action, and it is essential to navigating the terrain of your ambitions successfully.

To illustrate this concept with a relatable example, consider someone training for a marathon. The ultimate goal, or summit, is to complete the marathon. For many, this can seem overwhelming, especially if they've never run long distances before. But breaking it down into smaller, achievable steps makes it more manageable. Their first goalpost might be to run a 5K without stopping. The next mile marker could be increasing their distance to 10K, then to a half marathon, and so on. Each of these milestones represents progress on the path toward the summit. This is actually exactly how I made it from imitating a throw pillow on my sofa to running in the LA marathon. I cannot wait to run it again, hopefully without breaking my ankle this time. At least I was stubborn (dumb?) enough to go ahead and finish the race. No DNF for me!

Engagement with any aspect of your life, whether it's a goal, a value, or even a fear, becomes more meaningful and manageable when you give it a name. Naming something allows you to conceptualize it, making it tangible and, therefore, easier to address. For example, when you name your values, you bring them to the forefront of your consciousness, making it easier to live in alignment with them. Similarly, naming your fears diminishes their power by eliminating the fear of the unknown. The unknown is daunting because it's uncharted territory, but once you name your adversary, you gain control over it, reducing its influence on your life.

Naming your feelings, actions, and goals also engages a powerful cognitive tool called the reticular activating system (RAS). The RAS is a network of neurons in your brainstem that plays a crucial role in regulating wakefulness and attention. It acts as a filter for the vast amount of information your brain processes daily, helping you focus on what you consider important. For instance, if you're shopping for a specific car model, you might suddenly notice that model everywhere. It's not that the car has suddenly become more popular; rather, your RAS has started to filter out other stimuli to bring this car to your attention.

This same process applies to your goals. When you set your intentions by naming and focusing on your goals, your RAS begins to filter the information you encounter, highlighting opportunities, resources, and connections that can help you achieve your objectives. It's like setting your brain on autopilot to seek out the things that will bring you closer to your summit, even when you're not consciously thinking about it.

To harness the power of your RAS, I recommend a daily practice of writing down 10 affirmations in the present tense in your journal. These affirmations should reflect the outcomes you desire as if they've already been achieved. For example, if your goal is to write a book, one of your affirmations could be, "I am a published author." (See what I did there?) By consistently writing these affirmations, you're training your RAS to focus on and seek out the conditions and opportunities that will bring these affirmations to life.

Some might call this process "manifesting your desires." While the term "manifesting" can carry connotations of woo-woo or wishful thinking, it's important to understand that this practice is about much more than just positive thinking. It's about priming your mind to recognize and seize opportunities that align with your goals. Manifesting in this context is not a shortcut or a magical solution but rather a cognitive tool that aids you in the process of achieving your dreams. It's about directing your thoughts and actions toward your goals, ensuring that your mind is constantly working, even subconsciously, to bring you closer to your summit.

Consider the marathon runner again. As they progress through their training, they might visualize crossing the finish line, hearing the crowd cheer, and feeling the medal placed around their neck. This visualization isn't just daydreaming—it's priming the RAS to recognize that these images are goals to be achieved. Each training run, each increase in distance, is a step closer to turning that vision into reality.

As you progress toward your summit, it's crucial to understand that your journey will follow a specific structure, regardless of the goal. Your path will always include a starting line, mile markers, goalposts, and a finish line. This structure is your map, and having a well-defined map is key to navigating the journey ahead. The following chapters will delve deeper into the process of creating your map, ensuring you have a clear and actionable plan for achieving even the most ambitious goals.

By taking the time to define your map, you're setting yourself up for success. Each goal, no matter how grand or modest, becomes achievable when you break it down into manageable steps. With your map in hand, you can confidently approach your journey, knowing you have a clear path to follow. As you move from one summit to the next, you'll find that each journey not only brings you closer to your goals but also strengthens your resolve, sharpens your skills, and deepens your understanding of what you're truly capable of achieving.

In the end, the process of naming, mapping, and manifesting your goals is about taking control of your life's narrative. You're not just a passenger on this journey; you're the author of your story. By giving names to your goals, values, and challenges, you're scripting a life that is intentional, purposeful, and uniquely yours. With each summit you reach, you're achieving your goals and building a legacy of success and fulfillment that will continue to inspire you and those around you for years to come.

CHAPTER 18 – GET SMARTER

Now that you know better who you are as a person, have written out what you stand for, and defined the resources available to ease the struggles as you work toward your goals; you are ready to cartograph your map. First, you will need to determine your goal and what success in your goal looks like.

Now it is time to pick your goal. Grab a piece of paper and a pen. Start by listing out all your goals. Take a few minutes and write them all down. Don't think about whether or not they are too big or too small, real or imaginary, or whatever hierarchy they may be in your head. Put them all on the page. Seriously. Write them all. Include retiring at 45, vacation in Bora Bora, that goofy tattoo that will make you giggle daily, painting the half bath, a weekend with your girls, mowing the yard, and EVERYTHING else that you can think of that you want to accomplish someday.

Once you have your goals listed, you will organize them into a couple of categories. Are there any goals that can be combined or must be completed in chronological order to be reached? For instance, you can combine the following goals into cohesive groupings: Buy a house. Complete a triathlon. Learn to swim. Start working at home. Own a Schwinn bicycle. Let's say that you want to buy yourself a new Schwinn bicycle as a reward for completing the triathlon, but you cannot complete the tri until you learn to swim. Maybe you can start working remotely. This allows you to buy a house with the money you save by not commuting 5 days a week. You also have extra time to take swimming lessons in the morning because you are not going to be driving to the office. In this case, your goal grouping complements the potential for multiple successes. Obviously, this is a pretty simple example. I just want you to see how some goals relate to others. Remember that by working on one goal, you are really working on all of your goals.

This list is your goal bucket list. Your goal bucket list is a living document. It will grow and change with you as you cross off completed goals and add new ones. You will want to keep this list where it is easily accessible and editable. Perhaps an Excel spreadsheet or in a notes app on your phone. Your bucket list becomes a tangible record of your progress that you can refer to in times of struggle or disappointment to renew your spirits and inspire motivation to keep you moving forward. Adding a completed check or date to your list is a great way to see how much you have accomplished as you continue working on new goals.

Once you have all the goals that you can possibly think of organized on your list, you will pick the one goal you want to accomplish now. When you have The One, you will define the roadmap to success. The more specific you can be defining your goals, the more likely you are to succeed at them. You need a baseline and uniform way to define the path to achieving each of your goals. A good goal follows a defined structure, such as the SMART, PACT, or CLEAR methods. SMART goals are Specific, Measurable, Attainable, Relevant/realistic, and Time-bound. PACT stands for Purposeful, Actionable, Continuous, and Trackable. CLEAR goals are Collaborative, Limited, Emotional, Appreciable, and Refinable. I am going to focus on the SMART method in this chapter in an attempt to be less confusing. There are many methods to structure your goals. Use the one that feels right for you, or splice pieces of multiple methods into what works best for how your mind works. No one way is correct for everyone. The point is just that you can consistently create an actionable blueprint for each of your goals. When defining your goal, be as specific as possible. I cannot stress this enough. The goal on your list may be fairly vague at first. That is ok to start with. Work it into a clear and defined goal with one of these methods. Go over it a few times until you have met all the criteria. (For goals that are hard to set a timeline, focus on time within the mile markers rather than on the final outcome.)

Starting with the right definition is a major determining factor in how successful you will be. An example of a poorly written goal is "I want to get fit.". That's pleasantly vague enough to not be achievable. What does it even mean to get fit? How would you know if you reach your goal? This type of vagueness is a dream squasher. If you get more specific, the goal becomes more attainable. Instead of "I want to get fit", try "I want to be able to deadlift 100 lbs by my next birthday.". Do you feel the difference? Do you hear how the latter example is a SMART goal? It is specific. It is measurable because you can work your way up to 100 lbs. It is attainable because people deadlift even more weight than that all the time. It is realistic because you know how much you can deadlift now, and you have determined that increasing to 100 lbs is a reasonable weight-lifting goal. And it is time-bound because you have a date by which you want to accomplish this goal.

Then you want to write out your SMART goal into an affirmation. An affirmation is a sentence made up of powerful words put together into a positive and present tense statement with the intent to motivate and challenge you to reach your potential. An example of turning this goal into an affirmation is "I can deadlift 100 lbs.". You do not need to include the deadline because you want to bring it into the present tense. You want to write it as though it is already true. Turning your goals into affirmations is key to using your RAS, reticular activation system, to your advantage.

Another example of a poorly written goal is "I want to write a book.". Again, this is too vague to achieve. You could turn this into a SMART goal by changing it to "I will write a 50,000-word sci-fi book within 6 months.". This version is very specific. It is measurable because you can divide up how many words you need every week or day in order to reach the goal. You know it is attainable because there are many other sci-fi books around the same length in the world already. It is realistic because you can divide it into reasonably sized sections to make progress within the time frame. And it is time-based because you have the goal of completing it in 6 months.

If we tweak this goal a little bit you can see how the time-bound piece might not be in your control. If you change it to "I will write a best-selling 50,000-word sci-fi novel." It is still specific, measurable, attainable, and realistic. The difference is you cannot control when it will become a best seller. In cases like this, you will want to focus on putting a deadline on your goalposts and milemarkers in order to continue moving forward toward your goals in a timely manner. You could set a timeline for writing a certain number of words, completing, and publishing dates for the novel instead of putting a timeline on becoming a best seller. And the affirmation would be "My sci-fi novel is a best-seller.". Simple. Concise. And in the present tense.

Do you see how getting detailed in the language you use to define your goals can drastically change the outcome when striving for a goal? Using one of these methods to lay the foundation for your journey to success for every goal is just the beginning. Now that you have refined your goal, it's time to outline and organize your roadmap to success. In the next chapter, we will create the road map that will guide you to your dreams.

CHAPTER 19 – GOALPOSTS, MILE MARKERS, AND OBSTACLES. OH, MY!

Embarking on any journey toward success begins with a vision—a clear destination that you aim to reach. Whether you're striving for personal growth, professional achievement, or a significant life change, the process remains the same: you need a map to guide you. But unlike a physical map that charts well-worn paths, the map to your goal is uniquely your own, tailored to your specific ambitions and challenges. It's more than just a plan; it's a dynamic strategy that evolves with each step you take. In this chapter , we'll explore the essential steps to creating this map—a reliable framework that, when followed, turns the daunting process of goal-setting into an inevitable march toward success. With these steps, you're not just hoping to reach your destination—you're ensuring it. So, as you prepare to chart your course, remember that success is not a distant dream but a certain outcome when you follow the right path.

Though every map will be unique to the goal, the process of creating that map remains constant. No matter the destination or the challenge ahead, you will always rely on the same four foundational steps to chart your course. These steps are simple, but they are powerful. First, pick your goal—identify that summit you're striving for. Second, define the five-ish key actions or milestones that will guarantee your success in reaching that goal. Third, back-plan—work backward from your end goal to outline the steps required to get there. And finally, take at least one actionable step toward your goal every single day. This framework is your blueprint for success, a methodical approach that makes success not just possible but inevitable. Imagine what you could accomplish if you knew, with absolute certainty, that you would succeed. It's time to map out the journey to achieve it, by envisioning what success looks like for your specific goal, determining the five or so critical steps that will lead you there, and identifying the obstacles that might stand in your way. You'll then plot your path to success, fully aware of the potential challenges, and ready to overcome them.

As with any worthwhile endeavor, there will be bumps along the road, and it's important to anticipate these before diving headfirst into your plan. By acknowledging the potential obstacles now, you can develop strategies to sidestep or overcome them when they arise. Start by asking yourself: What are the possible barriers that could hinder your progress? What challenges could arise at any stage of your journey? These obstacles can be anything from time constraints and lack of resources to fears and self-doubt. If it worries you, it's worth considering. Take some time to write down everything that could go wrong—yes, everything. Don't hold back. Fill an entire page with your doubts, fears, and potential setbacks, from the practical to the improbable.

Once you have your list, it's time to categorize these obstacles into two groups: real and imaginary. Real obstacles are those challenges that are likely to occur and could genuinely impede your progress. Imaginary obstacles, on the other hand, are those that are unlikely to materialize but still occupy space in your mind. You might find that some of your imaginary obstacles have a basis in reality, but you've blown them out of proportion, like the fear of Aunt Wanda jaw flapping her critical opinions of everyone at the family reunion….Again. Now that you've sorted your obstacles, it's time to take action. Cross off any that are purely imaginary or irrational. Be honest with yourself here. We both know you're not going to encounter a radioactive spider or be chased out of the office by the Stay Puft Marshmallow Man. While these fears may make decent plot points in theatres, they aren't based in reality. In your life these are irrational fears, and they are a misuse of your creative energy. We don't waste time on irrational fears in this process.

With your list refined, it's time to confront the real obstacles head-on. Here's where we flip the script. The first thing I do every single time I face a new obstacle in life is to rename it. As I've mentioned before, naming something gives it form and makes it manageable. But I don't call them obstacles—I call them "opportunities." This intentional shift in perspective transforms a roadblock into a stepping stone. I first learned this approach on a memorable first date. My date told me that they had learned many ways not to succeed in a relationship, so they wanted to take this opportunity to try succeeding with me. Although the relationship didn't work out, that moment of intentional perspective change stuck with me. I knew then that I would need to share this insight in my work. Being intentional at every step, even when facing "obstacles," will propel you toward your goals faster, like hopping onto one of those moving walkways at the airport.

When most people encounter something negative, like an obstacle, their instinct is to run from it. They avoid it, procrastinate, and circle around it, often for far too long. They pretend it's not there, like ignoring the 800-pound gorilla in the room. But imagine all the time and energy you'll save by renaming that negative into a positive—by transforming your problems into integral parts of the solution. This shift in mindset is not just about positive thinking; it's about rescripting your challenges into opportunities for growth. Every obstacle reframed is another step closer to your summit, another victory on your path to success.

Next, rename your obstacles. Rewrite each one into a statement of potential progress instead of the potential problem. For example,

> Imaginary – "I don't have enough money to advertise."
> Real – "I don't know how to advertise without money."
> Rescripted - "I will look up three free ways to advertise."
> or
> Imaginary – "I need 1 million followers on social media."
> Real – "I need a better understanding of how to market with social media."
> Rescripted – "I will watch YouTube videos on marketing through my preferred social media site."

By turning your fears inside out, you have started the next step: Defining your goals. Each "rescripted obstacle" is now a mile-maker on your path. On a new page, write out all these new opportunities in the order that seems most chronologically effective order. Don't feel like you must get these in the exact order. A rough idea is enough right now. Save these inside-out obstacles for use in the coming exercises.

Are you feeling more in control now? Good!

Once you have the SMART goal to be accomplished, determined, and have rescripted any problems that could have gotten in the way, you will pick the 3-5 tasks that mean success. What 5 things, if completed, would guarantee you are reaching this goal? These 5 or so steps are your goalposts for your map. Your goalposts are like mini goals. You do not need to know exactly how to reach each goal post yet.

For example, if your goal is to go on a two-week vacation to Thailand, you would write down all the things you need to do to make this trip come to fruition. Your list may look like "pick travel dates," "book travel and accommodations," "look up things to do while you are there and important laws for tourists to know," "get your passport and travel visa," and "save money." These are your goalposts. Goal posts are steps to a summit that, if met, guarantee completion of your summit. Said another way. If you complete every step, you will succeed.

Next, it is time to back plan. Back planning is a technique for time management, a sort of reverse engineering, in which an individual starts at the metric for success and moves backward through time, noting the steps and time frames in reverse order. It is literally a backward path or timeline. For some of you, this concept may seem a bit counterintuitive. I assure you that back planning will help you see the bigger picture in more manageable pieces. It is used to break a goal down into an actionable timeline. You focus on your destination first and work backward to the starting line.

Just like you eat an elephant one bite at a time, your goals will be met if you take one step at a time. When I was in grade school, I always did the mazes in my Highlights Magazines backward. I'm not sure when I started doing them backward, but I figured out this was the most efficient way to find the correct path. If you go from the starting line, there are many wrong turns that you can make. However, if you start at the end, you limit the number of mistakes that are possible to make. In my 9th-grade art class, we learned to make a photo-realistic drawing by dividing the photo into a grid, covering all the squares except the one you were working on, and drawing it upside down. This broke the photo into small enough pieces so as to not be intimidating, even to those of us with the least experience or skill in drawing. By learning to start at the end and to work on things upside down and one piece at a time, I learned the concepts in this book at a young age. It took many years to realize the impact of these skills and even a few more years to be able to put them into cohesive thoughts for this book.

To back plan for success, you start at the realization of your goal, and you work in reverse, listing the steps that it takes to get to where you would begin. List out your goal posts in reverse chronological order leaving space between each post to add mile markers. Then, think, "What needs to happen for each step to become a reality?". Ask yourself this repeatedly until you no longer can find any actionable task that is required before you can complete said goal post. You can brainstorm on a sheet of paper to gather all the possible mile markers. Write down everything you can think of that could get you to your goalpost. Once you have them written out, go over them to cull out anything that can be combined into another action, or that is just busy work.

These tasks to reach your goalposts are your mile markers. They are what you will be doing as you work toward your goalposts every day. You can have as many mile markers between your goalposts as necessary. List as many as you think it will take to reach each goal post. Mile markers are how you begin to make forward motion and build momentum to reach your goals. They can be daily tasks that need to be completed to make the time to work on your goals or micro goals themselves. They can be conversations with someone who can help or google research on the information you need to reach other steps along the way. Your mile markers are the smaller but tangible tasks that really do add up when it comes to working toward your dreams.

Be careful not to get lost in the busy work, thinking that you are making progress. This is easy to slip into without the proper planning. By listing out your mile markers, you can prevent this time-wasting behavior. Defining your mile markers also helps prevent the feeling of overwhelm that can accompany reaching for larger goals. You can prioritize and label everything that needs to be done so there is no confusion on where to begin, which is often what creates the overwhelm in the first place.

When you complete a mile marker, you know you are one more step closer to your goalposts. Passing each mile marker along your path not only gives you a tangible sense of progress but also allows you to build momentum along the way. As I have mentioned before, often getting started is the hardest part of any goal. I believe that not knowing the location of your starting line is often the biggest deterrent to starting in the first place. Just like when planning a drive to somewhere new, you must know where you are beginning your trip as well as the final destination in order to find the correct directions to get you there. By back planning, you can discover the starting location. You may recall the proverb that the journey of 10,000 miles begins with one step. It's true. The more often you take that first step, the easier they will become. By breaking your goals down into bite-size pieces, you can measurably climb toward your summit regularly.

After you have all your mile markers written down, organize them into groups. You want them grouped with the goal post they will be most effective in assisting to complete. Remember to add in the obstacles that you reconstructed into mile markers earlier. They will give you courage as you reach outside of your comfort zone to accomplish your goals.

Once you have the back plan for your goal, you will write it out in chronological order. In this example, your path would look something like this:

Starting line- Pick a date to travel

Goal post 1- Get a current passport

- Print passport application
- Take passport photos
- Send in the application and fee

Goal post 2- Give employer or clients notice of time away from work

- Write out a letter of intent
- Turn into a supervisor or send to clients

Goal post 3- look up info about Thailand

- Look up things to do in Thailand
- Look up the weather in Thailand
- Look up laws that tourists should be aware of in Thailand

Goal post 4- Save money for the trip

- Open a savings account just for the trip
- Determine how much to save each week
- Find little ways to save extra

Goal post 5- Book trip and travel visa

- Go to Dr for any necessary vaccinations for travel
- Book hotel
- Book flights

- Book rental car
- Buy tickets to any events that you want to attend while in Thailand
- Pack bags

Finish line – Go to Thailand

Affirmation – I had a great 2-week vacation in Thailand!

Let's consider another example. This time let's look at a life goal of completing a race. In this example, we will discuss how specific to be when picking a goal, how to activate your RAS with purpose, and back plan your map to success.

Poor example: I want to run a triathlon.

Better example: I want to finish an Ironman race.

Best example: I will finish the next Los Angeles Ironman Race in under 14 hours.

The last example is a SMART goal. Now let's build a map to reach the goal.

The summit is the literal Finish Line of the race. Because the Ironman is a triathlon, 3 of the goalposts are to be able to swim 2.4 miles, run a marathon, and ride a bicycle 112 miles. Another goalpost could be to qualify for the race. And finally, let's say you need to learn to swim.

For the goal of running the next Ironman in less than 14 hours, you know you need to learn to swim, train to swim 2.4 miles, train for a marathon, qualify for the specific race you want to run, train to cycle for over a hundred miles, and time yourself to ensure a 14-hour completion. Now organize these in reverse chronological order as follows:

Summit- Reach the finish line.

Goal post 5- qualify for the race

Goal post 4- run at least 26.2 miles without stopping

Goal post 3- cycle at least 112 miles without stopping

Goal post 2- swim at least 2.4 miles without stopping

Goal post 1- learn to swim

Starting line- I will finish the Los Angeles Ironman in under 14 hours next year.

Affirmation- I finished the Los Angeles Ironman in 13 hours and 24 minutes.

Next, you are going to list your mile markers for each post. The mile markers are the steps that get you from one goalpost to the next. Break them into the smallest tasks you can. Every goalpost should have at least 3 tasks that you can complete to guarantee that you reach the goalpost. Are you seeing the pattern here? (Thank you, reticular activator.) If you think of the biggest goal as your summit, the goalposts are mini goals, and the mile markers are micro goals. If you struggle to define the mile markers for a goalpost, use the same process that you used to break the summit into the initial goalposts. Do this breakdown until you have enough mile markers to reach each goalpost. Some goalposts will have many mile markers, while some will only have a few. You aren't doing it wrong if this is the case. Remember that every path is different. Some steps are easier than others.

After back-planning the goal posts and mile markers, you reverse the order so that you have a forward chronologically ordered path from where you are to success, the summit. This is your map! You have it now. You are ready to move into realizing your goals.

Mark Twain once basically said, "If you must eat a frog, do it in the morning. If you must eat two, eat the big one first.". I took this to heart. I decided to always do the things that scare me first. Get the scary stuff out of the way so I can focus on the fun stuff.

I employed this technique when I decided to become a trucker. Yes, the big ones. I have a CDL class A driver's license, and I am not afraid to use it. Obtaining the license was pretty scary, though. As you already know, I am an all-or-nothing sort of person. However, this was the first time I was consciously implementing the ideas I didn't yet know were for this book. I was about to eat the frogs.

I had just gone through a truly rough divorce that left me and my daughter living out of my vehicles and nearly bankrupt in Minneapolis, MN. Thankfully, one of them was an RV, but let me tell you that the winters are no joke up there. There were several times we had to get a hotel room because it was too cold in the RV. My daughter was in her junior year of high school, and I was working as a manager at Starbucks. I knew we both couldn't keep this up. I was up at 3 am on a Tuesday with my best friend, anxiety. What better time to watch YouTube videos of people living their dreams? I came across a video of a woman who had a similar situation to ours. She was explaining how she became a trucker. In the video, she said that she received a grant through the state to get women into male-dominated careers. I, of course, went straight to Google. I was able to find a grant. At 8:00 am, while on my lunch break at Starbucks, I called Angela with the state career office to ask about the grant. She informed me that not only was she about to close the grant for the year, but there were also three other women in front of me with only 1 spot available. After some discussion (read pleading), she told me that if there was still a spot available and I had my CDL permit by the following Friday, she would add me to the grant. After my coffee-slinging shift, I went straight to the DMV.

I was able to call Angela back the very next morning and tell her that I had my permit. Friday came and I was added to the grant. Once I had signed all the paperwork, I put in my two weeks' notice at Starbucks deciding to live off the tiny amount that I had saved in my 401k. Almost 5 weeks later and getting low on cash, I passed my CDL test on the very first try. I now knew that my idea was successful. If you do the things, you reach the goal. It really is that simple. Simple not easy. And I only had to eat a few frogs.

Taking the big risks can also be scary. I took a huge risk walking away from a full-time job knowing quite well that I wouldn't be paid again for at least six weeks. I knew everything would have to go exactly as planned to even get a paycheck then. I'm pleased to tell you that everything went just right, and that first paycheck came *on my birthday*. Too often we don't take big risks because we focus on what could go wrong. Worrying is like a rocking chair; it gives you something to do but you won't get anywhere. I say, if you are going to use your imagination anyway, you might as well imagine the good things happening instead. Do not misuse your imagination. That is abuse of the self and we don't do that here!

If you are thinking about taking a life-changing risk, it is much more likely to be a successful endeavor if you believe that to be the case. You are more likely to find a solution to the problems that inevitably arise if you practice believing in what you can do instead of what you cannot. Remember that you can decide what your Reticular Activating System focuses on. Let it help you! Believe you will succeed.

Now you have the goal decided. You have determined what your goalposts are that will lead you to success. And you have discovered all the mile markers that will push you along the way to the realization of your goal. Congratulations. This is your path to achieving your goal. You now have the exact road to take, complete with goalposts and mile markers to keep you motivated and let you gauge when adjustments become necessary. If you complete all these steps, you will reach your goal of going to Thailand, finishing a triathlon, or any other goal you can dream up. Whatever your personal goals are, if you design your life around a map like this, you will build the life of your dreams.

CHAPTER 20 - LIMITING BELIEFS

You already know how SMART goals help you define your path and keep you on track in many ways. You can even fight off that negative self-talk that sneaks into our lives by using the combination of SMART goal setting and the mapping technique together. When I first tell clients that they can set themselves up in a way that ensures success, often they will start telling me some of the things they actually can't do. Often, they will have a problem for every solution. These are their limiting beliefs.

A limiting belief is a self-imposed limit to what you allow yourself to accomplish. Yes, it is a *self-imposed limit to your potential*. Many people struggle with these limiting beliefs, so much that it can hinder their future successes. You will want to be aware of your own limiting belief system as you reach for your dreams. You will be able to recognize a limiting belief by how it makes you feel small in your own world. Anytime you hear yourself say, "I am not worthy of...", "I could never do/have...", "I am not _____ enough.", or anything with "I can't...." or "I should...", take a moment to examine the fears associated with these statements. A limiting belief is an embodiment of your fears. Fears and worries are theoretically designed to keep us safely tucked into our cocoon of a comfort zone. Most often, when you are taking a risk or working toward a goal, you are reaching beyond your comfort zone. Your imagination comes up with many reasons why you might fail. This is an abuse of your imagination and a waste of time. Instead of imagining failures, imagine successes. Instead of "What if I fall?" say "What if I fly?". Rescripting your life can have a profound impact on whether or not you succeed and the energy it takes to bust free from your cozy chrysalis to experience the growth necessary to reach your wildest dreams.

You only experience fears when you stay locked inside your comfort zone. Growth and success only happen outside of your comfort zone. Once you decide to leave the fear and relative safety inside your comfort zone you then can experience the courage that is waiting for you on the outside. Catching yourself in a limiting belief mindset can be proof you are heading in the right direction. When you notice a limiting belief is present, see it and rebuke it immediately. Often the obstacles we fear are part of the path. "The obstacle is the way," as Ryan Holiday says. We know we are passing out of our comfort zones when the fears and obstacles start to appear. Keep pushing through to your courage. I wanna see you be brave. Growth is right around the corner.

There have been several times when I was afraid to do the one thing that would make the biggest difference at the time. You've heard me mention it before, but here is the full quote. Mark Twain said, "If it's your job to eat a frog, it's best to eat it in the morning. And if it's your job to eat two frogs, it's best to eat the biggest one first." Thanks to that quote, I decided to do whatever was scaring me immediately. "Just eat the damn frog!" isn't a mantra you will hear from many other vegans.

One time that eating the frog made all the difference was while I was training to become a trucker. I had told the directors that I was living in an RV that was parked about 5 minutes away, so if anyone didn't show up for practice, to please let me know, and I would come in their place as I was trying to get my license as quickly as I could. One morning I got the call to go practice driving on the street. Instantly, I was excited and nervous. It was me and 4 men. Our instructor that day asked who wanted to go first. This was the last step I needed before I could take the actual driver's license test. So, I ate the frog and volunteered to go first. Thank goodness I did because the gentleman who followed me ended up breaking the practice truck, and it was down for 2 weeks. I had my CDL before that truck was fixed. Had I let the fear control me and waited, I would have run out of money before I got licensed. I wouldn't tell you to eat the frog if it wasn't worth it.

Eating the frog is one way to combat limiting beliefs. Affirmations and mantras can also help you overcome your limitations. Fear of failure, success, rejection, or not being worthy are some very common limiting beliefs. You can address these by adding affirmations to your daily routine. That can look like telling yourself that you are worthy of love and respect regularly. I started by writing on my bathroom mirror that I deserved to be loved well and would read it repeatedly while brushing my teeth. Another way to combat these feelings is to chant a mantra that is triggered by the negative belief. I use mantras during meditations and while running all the time. When I feel myself thinking I could finish my run early, I just repeat, "I am strong. Be strong" or "Can't stop. Won't stop" until I believe in my ability to complete my run. Sometimes that means repeating my mantras all the way over the finish line.

I feel like my imposter syndrome was born out of limiting beliefs. Imposter syndrome makes you feel undeserving of your achievements. It can make you feel as though you are a fraud, even in areas in which you are objectively and quantitatively capable. I feel obligated to warn you that the next sentence is going to sound a bit unhinged, but it is unequivocally true. Kid Rock cured my imposter syndrome. I am fully aware of how bizarre that is. Let me explain. I was lost somewhere in the depths of the internet, and mid-doom scroll, I happened upon an article that was calling out Kid Rock for not quite having the blue-collar, trailer trash background that he would have you believe. It had images of the McMansion he grew up in and him in his Vanilla Ice era. Don't get me wrong, I understand that not all that glitters is gold and Hollywood is full of smoke and mirrors. That said, reading that article made it click for me. If Kid Rock can make millions being a literal imposter, then I can do anything. I even half-ass know what I'm doing sometimes. If he can successfully pretend to be a down-home working man, I can do anything I can dream of too. And so can you, limiting beliefs be damned.

CHAPTER 21 - MOTIVATION REVISITED

Motivation is defined by Merriam-Webster as the condition of being eager to act or work. The problem is motivation is a fickle creature. Some days, it's there strong, and other days, you don't want to do anything. This is normal. Everyone struggles to be motivated from time to time. Dr. Julie Smith writes that motivation comes after the action in her book Why Has Nobody Told Me This Before?. This concept explains why our motivation would wane at times when our feelings about the project haven't changed. If you want to feel like doing something, you must do it first. While it seems counterintuitive at first glance, it makes more sense the longer you look at it. How many times have you dreaded doing something, like going for the long run that week, just to be excited and reenergized afterward? This is how you can gain momentum easier than you can find your motivation.

It may seem as though some people have being motivated hard-wired into their normal operating systems. I wish I was one of those people. I, personally, struggle with motivation on the daily. Yay, depression! And ADHD! And ASD! (Go team?! Face palm) Because of this, I have learned how to "life hack" myself. Mel Robbins' 5-second rule was a game-changer for me. If you ever struggle with motivation, put this book on your "to read" list. I also struggle with executive dysfunction when I'm having a particularly bad round of auDHD symptoms or a "fibro flare". Executive dysfunction is a range of cognitive, behavioral, or emotional difficulties that occur as a result of a traumatic brain injury or, in my case, as a result of another disorder. Someone with executive dysfunction may struggle with planning, organization, and time management. When I am having a really difficult time coping with my executive dysfunction, I implement the 5-second rule.

In a nutshell, the 5-second rule requires that, no matter what, after you count down from 5 you must do the thing you are avoiding or don't want to do. Often it is the starting that is the problem. Once you are in motion, you will keep going. Unless a squirrel knocks on the front door again. The 5-second rule allows me, and hopefully, you, to get moving toward my goal without the motivation that would typically drive me to get a move on. Again, motivation comes after action. This is why, if you convince yourself to just sit down and write for 15 minutes, you can end up writing for 3 hours and making a ton of progress. Or why when you start a load of laundry, you might also become motivated to sweep and mop "while you're at it". The motivation that you create by starting the very thing you are procrastinating breeds a great deal of momentum. You may have "gotten into a grove" or "found your flow". These are times that you create your motivation. Because you "might as well" get some other important shit done while you're doing the important shit.

Sometimes, the issue holding you back may not be a lack of motivation. Maybe, like the hamster, you are too involved in running on your wheel to realize you aren't going anywhere. You might need to regroup and step back from what you are doing to reexamine the big picture. Too often, we get lost working "in" our goals that we forget to work "on" them.

We know that motivation isn't something you are just born with or without. This means that you can do things that lessen or generate motivation. Thanks to Sir Isaac Newton, we know that a body in motion will stay in motion. If you keep this in mind as you ponder motivation, it is easy to deduce that lying around and procrastinating will only assist you in lying around and procrastinating.

The way to get motivated is quite simple, then. You fake it 'til you make it, baby. That's right. If you want to be motivated, get up and pretend you are. And maybe grab an espresso con panna on the way. When you catch yourself procrastinating or wishing you were working on your goals, set a timer for 15 minutes and do just that. Manifest your motivation and build your momentum.

Ok. Seriously though, there will be times that you do not want to do the thing. Count down from 5, set the timer for 15 minutes, and start doing the thing you definitely do not want to be doing right now. If at the end of the fifteen minutes, you still don't want to be doing it, then stop. But, if when your timer dings, you feel as though you were just getting started, keep going. Find the motivation hidden within the actions you are taking toward your goal. If you do this every day that you are struggling to get started on your mile marker, you will find yourself knocking your goalposts out of the park and reaching summit after summit, faster than you could have ever imagined. This is because you are building momentum. Momentum breeds motivation. You will literally become motivated by the momentum you create by forcing yourself to get up and just do the damn thing.

As a matter of fact, this is the exact technique that I used, and continue to use, to write this book. I had all these ideas for chapters in my head but no clue how to get them onto paper. I decided to spend just 15 minutes working on a brainstorm map. This turned into a couple of hours and an organized outline. The outline thankfully gives me the structure to come back to wherever in the book that I feel excited to write about each day. (Side note: the squirrel brain plus fibro fog is how I accidentally wrote 2 chapters on motivation, but I am so glad it worked like this. But hey, I'll take a win when I can!) If I am not feeling excited about writing, I'll go back and reread it, editing as I go, until I feel moved to write. The *starting* is always the hardest part. 5,4,3,2,1…. GO!

CHAPTER 22 – THE END

Now it is time to do the damn thing. You have put in the work to get this far. You have looked deep within yourself to find who you are inside and out. You reflected on your personal convictions to determine what exactly you stand for. You have your ethics and mission written in black and white. You have all your resources within arm's reach. Your mentors are a guiding light on your journey. You know who has your six and where to find support. You have defined what success means for you and mapped the road to it. You are ready to take the next step.

What happens now that you have reached the jumping-off point? Ask yourself, "What can I do now?". Yes, right now. What could you do at this moment that would make you feel invested in your goal? This can mean anything that gets you fired up and ready to move forward. Your investment can be monetary, educational, physical, or emotional. Unfortunately, it is common when you are first reaching toward a goal to be tempted to only take a teeny, tiny step. Society has conditioned us to believe that it is better to just get your feet wet and see if you like it. You think you should just take a moment to dip your toe in instead of jumping right in. This is a form of indecision. Indecision is a form of self-abuse. By choosing to be small, you are cheating yourself. We don't do that here!

You have spent time building a foundation for success in your goals. Think back through everything you have done in this book. Think of all the work you have put in already. Yes, you might be looking to complete the very first mile marker on your map for the very first time, but you must remember you have been working toward all your goals by preparing to get to this step. You are clearly committed to your goals and the best thing you can do is swan dive off the deep end. Go for the gold. Start running headfirst for your biggest and wildest dreams. Grab life by the horns and get her done.

As you have heard probably a thousand times in your life, starting is the hardest part, but remember, the journey of 10,000 miles begins with one step. You may feel insecure that you aren't making the right moves. Have you ever used a GPS that thought you were facing the other direction when you started? You hear the dreaded "recalculating," but soon, the GPS understands where you are in relation to where you are going, and your path is clear. You will be able to course correct as often as needed once you are moving toward the goal. Taking massive action demonstrates to yourself that you have made the decision to be successful and are truly committed to achieving your desires. Getting started is a way to truly love yourself and say, "I am worthy. I deserve to be successful.".

One way to stay on track once you are working toward your goal is by assessing your results. Remember the T in SMART goals is time-bound. You will want to give yourself a timeline to complete each mile marker along your map. Perhaps, checking in on your progress weekly or biweekly is best for your goal. Set a reminder on your phone to check in on yourself regularly. When you reliably check how your actions are working, you are able to see when things are or aren't working as planned. This hindsight allows you to course correct much faster than if you just keep doing the same things and wasting time until you reach the mile marker. Ask yourself every day, "What did I learn? What went right? What could have gone better?". Set one day every week or two to review the answers to these daily questions. Reflect on your answers and goal strategy. Then assess what is working, what is not working, and what changes you could make to improve the process.

It is important to stay focused on the outcome when working toward your goals. You do not want to get too attached to the "how" of reaching them. Sometimes, everything might go as planned, but more likely than not, you will need to be flexible on your journey at some point. You are able to stay headed toward your goals while adjusting the path, just like your GPS does when you miss a turn, as needed if you assess the effectiveness of your strategies and progress regularly. There is no one right way to do anything. There may be dozens of ways to reach a goal, but only one way not to. You must never quit. If something doesn't work, try something new. DO NOT GIVE UP. Keep in mind that if part of the process isn't working as planned, that is not a reflection of you. It only means that the process needs an adjustment. The only true failure is to quit.

We are all on our own journey. We all have different summits and valleys in our mountain ranges. We have different habits, limiting beliefs, baggage, and other bullshit that will get in our way. We all start with different resources. At some point in our journeys, we may cross paths.

Remember that you are your only competition. Share as much of your journeys as you can with each other when you meet. You might learn something infinitely valuable for your future growth. And you never know; your words may be another's survival guide. Be kind, you don't know what they are going through. A small kindness from you may echo through every success they have. If your words can cut or cure, wouldn't you rather multiply the kindness in the world than cut down a peer into giving up? Be the change you want to see in the world, right?

We have been on quite the adventure together in these pages. Not as cool an adventure as Bilbo, but an adventure to a new you just the same. You have discovered more about yourself and defined what it is exactly that you stand, and won't stand, for. You have made a bucket list of goals that can grow with you. You have learned how to name your goals in a way that makes them attainable and to rename your fears into opportunities for growth and progress. You have determined what resources are available to assist you in reaching your goals. You know who is in your circle. Where to reach for support. You have found your mentors. You are aware of how and when to eat the frogs in your way. Most Importantly, you know that you can reach your goals with this knowledge.

Now you know how to reach all your goals. Pass go and collect $200. You can do anything. I cannot wait to see what ideas you bring into this world. Thank you for allowing me to be a part of your journey to becoming a basket case. You are ready. This is the inception of your journey to success. You have everything you need to reach for all of your goals, one basket at a time. I cannot wait to hear from you as you find your way to the life you want.

Yakoke for joining me in this journey. Congrats! You are officially a basket case. I am proud of you.

Go get'em, tiger!

Made in the USA
Columbia, SC
03 September 2024

9f4c709f-8014-494d-b2bb-bd5cb55c65a2R01